cashing it in

cashing it in

Getting Ready for a World Without Money

ETHAN POPE

MOODY
PUBLISHERS

CHICAGO

Certified Financial Planner Board of Standards Inc. owns the certification mark CERTIFIED FINANCIAL PLANNER™, which it awards to individuals who successfully complete the CFP Board's initial and ongoing certification requirements.

All Scripture quotations, unless otherwise indicated, are taken from the *New American Standard Bible*®, © Copyright The Lockman Foundation 1960, 1962, 1963, 1968, 1971, 1972, 1973, 1975, 1977, 1995. Used by permission.

Scripture quotations marked NIV are taken from the *Holy Bible, New International Version*®. NIV®. Copyright © 1973, 1978, 1984 by International Bible Society. Used by permission of Zondervan Publishing House. All rights reserved.

Scripture quotations marked NLT are taken from the *Holy Bible, New Living Translation,* copyright © 1996. Used by permission of Tyndale House Publishers, Inc., Wheaton, Illinois 60189. All rights reserved.

Scripture quotations marked NKJV are taken from the *New King James Version.* Copyright © 1982 by Thomas Nelson, Inc. Used by permission. All rights reserved.

Design: The DesignWorks Group; cover, Charles Brock; interior, Robin Black.
        www.thedesignworksgroup.com

ISBN: 0-8024-0971-7

LIBRARY OF CONGRESS CATALOGING-IN-PUBLICATION DATA

Pope, Ethan.
        Cashing it in : getting ready for a world without money / Ethan Pope.
              p.   cm.
        Includes bibliographical references.
        ISBN-13: 978-0-8024-0971-3
        1. Electronic funds transfers—Social aspects. 2. Finance, Personal—Religious aspects—Christianity. I. Title.
        HG1710.P67 2005
        303.48'33—dc22

                                                                            2005010773

1 3 5 7 9 10 8 6 4 2

Printed in the United States of America

table of contents

Acknowledgments 7

Introduction: **THE ALERT** 9
what will a cashless society mean for you?

Chapter 1: **THE EXPERIMENT** 14
Are you ready for a world without cash?

Chapter 2: **THE SIGNS** 22
is there any evidence we are close to becoming a cashless society?

Chapter 3: **THE TECHNOLOGY CONTROVERSY** . 46
what is RFID?

Chapter 4: **THE PRIVACY CONTROVERSY** 61
should I be concerned about anything?

Chapter 5: **THE BENEFITS** 78
Are there any benefits of living in a cashless society?

Chapter 6: **THE PREPARATION** 88
what should I be doing?

Chapter 7: **THE CAUTIONS** 101
what should I not be doing?

Chapter 8: **THE FORECAST** 114
what will the transition to and future in a cashless society look like?

Chapter 9: **THE PROPHECY** 124
is a cashless society a sign of the end of the world?

Chapter 10: **THE RESPONSE** 134
How can christians respond to concerns about a cashless society?

Chapter 11: **THE TWO WORLDS** 147
Are you ready for another world without money?

UPDATES 156
How can i keep up-to-date on critical issues concerning the cashless society?

THE CASHLESS TIME LINE 157

GLOSSARY 162

ABOUT THE AUTHOR 169

CONTACTING ETHAN POPE 170

acknowledgments and appreciation

Thank you . . .

Greg Thornton, for your partnership and most of all for your friendship. I am honored that you invited me to join the Moody Publisher team.

Bill Thrasher, for your enthusiasm and passion to see relevant financial books published. Keep the fire burning!

Allan Sholes, for your editing and gentle prodding to keep this book headed in the right direction.

To everyone at Moody Publishers who worked on this project. You are loved and appreciated. It's an honor to be on the same team with you.

Jay Gemes, Marcus Robinson, Mike Treat, and W. G. Miller for reading the original manuscript and being available to answer all my probing questions.

Jimmy Stewart, not only for reading the original manuscript, but for your friendship, words of encouragement, and our prayer time.

Ministry partners who are so faithful to pray for our ministry and support it financially.

Janet, Natalie, and Austin. I am blessed beyond measure to have such a wonderful wife, daughter, and son. A special thanks to Janet, who has the difficult task of being the first person to read everything I write. *I trust your reward in heaven will be great!*

INTRODUCTION

. . . .

The Alert

what will a cashless society mean for you?

ONE OF THE JOYS OF WRITING this book was spending time with many of my friends and associates discussing the coming cashless society. Together, we prayed, we laughed, we ate junk food, we looked at God's Word, and we challenged one another to live for Christ, no matter what the future brings—cash or cashless.

Let me share with you what I noticed over and over again during these candid conversations with my friends.

The more we talked about going cashless, the deeper the conversation became. The more questions they began asking, the more concerns they developed, and the more interested they became in learning what I had discovered about this topic—*especially if and how it relates to biblical prophecy.*

Like you and me and so many other consumers in our economy, they've sensed increasing pressures to go electronic and say good-bye to paper—whether cash, checks, or even statements. I could see them calculating, thinking, processing, and wondering, ***"What does a cashless society mean for my family?"***

9

I noticed that as we talked, many would actually lean forward in their chairs, indicating a deeper interest in this topic. On a few occasions, I would notice a look of concern or some nervous laughter as we talked.

I might add, a totally cashless society was a topic very few had ever thought about deeply before our conversation. But now it was blinking on their "radar screen" and demanding some thought and attention.

They started asking me penetrating questions, including their top concern, which I'll tell you in a moment. Let me give you a sampling:

- "How can I best prepare to live in a cashless society?"
- "Exactly what does the Bible say about a cashless society?"
- "How do you know it's going to happen? Do you have any proof?"
- "Ethan, what are the ramifications that concern you most?"
- "Are there any benefits to living in a cashless society?"
- "Will a cashless society be secure from fraud and identity theft?"
- "Is a cashless society technologically possible?"
- "What can we expect to happen over the next few years?"
- "What do I really need to know about a cashless society?"
- "What should our response be as Christians concerning the cashless society? Fight it? Ignore it? Promote it?"

- "How can I keep up-to-date on critical issues concerning the cashless society?"

But besides these, what do you think is the **number one question** most of them were asking me? Here it is:

"Ethan, does a cashless society mean we are near the end of the world?"

That's right! The number one question dealt with the last days of the world as we know it.

As you can see from the table of contents for this book, their questions, along with a survey I conducted and my research, helped to establish the framework for this book.

Do you find yourself interested in discovering the answers to these same questions? I trust the answer is yes.

If I were sitting across the table from you right now, here is what I would do. I would look right into your eyes, speak very slowly and say: *"Let me be very clear as I explain why this topic is so important."*

We are on the eve of one of the most significant economic developments in the history of the world ...

- The cashless society will change the way we live, give, invest, bank, buy, and sell.
- Every transaction will be exposed to digital eyes that will be able to trace your every financial move.
- The probability that your freedom and privacy can be invaded and abused will be at an all-time high.

- The potential for persecution will be at an all-time high if your personal data is ever controlled by radical anti-Christians.

- A cashless society will likely be a key aspect of a major biblical prophecy being fulfilled! We are one giant step closer to what is biblically known as the Great Tribulation.

- And finally, we're already on our way to becoming a cashless society.

If you weren't convinced that this is an important topic, are you now?

Whether you're convinced or not at this point, let me urge you to read and study this book. View it as a manual. Much of it is in a simple question-and-answer format to help you better understand the issues and know what you should and should not be doing. I am not sounding an *alarm*, but simply an *alert!*

As believers, one of our responsibilities is to be on the alert.

We are told at the end of Luke 21, "But keep on the alert at all times, praying in order that you may have strength to escape all these things that are about to take place."

1 Peter 5:8 instructs us to "be of sober *spirit*, be on the alert."

Webster defines *alert* as: "watchful and ready, as in facing danger."[1]

This book is a specific call for Christians to do just that—*be on the alert!*

We'll begin by looking at the financial aspects of a cashless society (new technologies, identity theft, security, and preparation). Then later in the book we'll spend time answering one of the most probing questions my friends were asking: ***"What does the Bible have to say about a cashless society?"***

You will see how I answered my friends' question about what the Bible has to say about a cashless society and if we are living in the last days.

---

[1] *Webster's New World Dictionary of the American Language,* 2nd college ed., s.v. "alert."

CHAPTER 1

The Experiment

Are you ready for a world without cash?

RECENT DEVELOPMENTS AND INDISPUTABLE SIGNS have overwhelmingly convinced me that we will be living in a cashless society within the next few years. Maybe not totally cashless, but virtually cashless in less than ten years! For practical, technological, and biblical reasons, I believe eventually all our cash will disappear. No more dollar bills, no more coins, no more checks!

Now is the time we should be getting ready for a world without money.

Over the years I have been somewhat of a "financial traditionalist." By that I mean I rarely used a credit card, I prolonged signing up for a debit card, avoided using the U-Scan checkout lane, never paid for gas at the pump using a credit card, never used an ATM, and under no circumstances made purchases on the Internet!

In the last few years, though, my financial life has radically changed! I don't know if it was as a result of (a) my age, forty-eight, (b) increasing wisdom, (c) stupidity,

14

or (d) simply seeing and understanding the benefits of cashless transactions for the first time. I hope the answer is (d). Whatever the reason, I now use a debit card, frequently use a credit card, use the U-Scan lane at every opportunity, make micropurchases (of less than five dollars) on my credit and debit cards, and consistently shun gas stations that don't offer the option to pay at the pump! And yes, now I even purchase items online using my debit and credit cards!

How drastic a change has this been in my life? For those who know me well, the change would be just as dramatic and shocking as if one day Fox News TV talk-show host Sean Hannity announced that he had become a Democrat and a card-carrying member of the American Civil Liberties Union, or if his cohost Alan Colmes announced that he was now a Republican and a card-carrying member of The Moral Majority Coalition.

What brought about such a radical change in the way I managed my finances and lived my life? *I realized that I needed to change or be left behind!* Here is how it all began…

"The" Debit Card

My introduction and moment of decision concerning the new economy happened when I went with my daughter, Natalie, to open her checking account. The banker posed a question that I was not prepared to answer: "Do you want Natalie to have a debit card?" After feeling mentally paralyzed for a few seconds, I gained my composure, turned to my firstborn, Natalie, and asked if she would like to have a debit card.

She sat stunned for a few seconds in disbelief that I was actually asking her if she wanted a debit card. I am sure she was thinking, *Wait a minute; is this really my dad? Is this really Ethan Pope, "Mr. Financial Traditionalist," asking me if I want a debit card?* I already knew the answer before I asked her. If you ever give a teenager the opportunity to have a colorful, rectangular, plastic card in her purse or wallet, you know the answer will be YES. But just to make it official, I asked, and just to make it official, she broke out in a big smile and said, "YES."

Natalie became the first Pope to own a debit card. I would have to say that this was a *major financial milestone* in our family that helped to bring about additional changes in my life that I never imagined would happen. Why had I never signed up for a debit card? I assume the best reason was I didn't like the idea of someone being able to take money "instantly and directly" out of my checking account.

A few months later, when my son, Austin, opened his checking account, accepting the debit card offer was a no-brainer! Of course he wanted a debit card! This is the twenty-first century! Don't you realize that checks are going the way of the dinosaur to extinction? According to various reports, the number of checks being written peaked in the mid-1990s and has been declining ever since. The moral of the story: *Change or be left behind.*

"The" Payment at the Pump

The second major change in my financial life took place when I made my first purchase of gas at the pump using a credit card. The simplicity was incredible. I inserted and quickly removed my card, pumped my gas, removed the printed receipt, put my receipt in my wallet, got in my car, and drove away. No walking inside, no waiting in line, and no signature required. One word comes to mind when I think about paying at the pump: *easy!*

Several years after that historic moment in my financial life, as I am writing about this story, I am thinking, *Why did I wait and protest paying at the pump for so many years? What was I fearful of? Why did I force myself always to go inside and stand in a long line to pay for my gas?*

My analysis: I had never done that before, and I was simply a skeptic of the new payment system. The bottom line: I lacked trust. But, of what? Why did I trust that the eighteen-year-old kid with blue hair, a ring in his nose, and more holes in his body than a used target at a shooting range, who was possibly hired and trained yesterday and earning minimum wage, would do a better job in processing my credit card transaction than I could? *Absolutely no logic!* I was acting like an old dog not wanting to learn a new trick. The moral of the story: *Change or be left behind.*

"The" Internet Purchase

The third major event in my financial progression was making my first purchase on the Internet. Why had I never done this before? It was simply a concern about the security aspect and not understanding how the system worked. Just as with most events in life, after you do something once, it becomes easier. To my surprise, the next credit card bill I received after making my Internet purchase was not for ten thousand dollars, as I feared would happen, but only for the ten dollar purchase I actually made. I guess I had seen too many television commercials about credit card fraud. You know, the ones where the man is talking like a woman or the woman is talking like a man.

I realize that people do get caught in the middle of credit card fraud, but in 99.9 percent of all Internet transactions, fraud is not involved. More on this topic later in the book. The moral of the story: *Change or be left behind.*

"The" U-Scan Aisle

Finally, I knew I had somewhat embraced (with caution) the new economy when I successfully used the U-Scan aisle at Wal-Mart. This was a *major* milestone in my life.

I had read about U-Scan and had even seen them at our local Wal-Mart store. I often thought that if I used the U-Scan lane I would be helping to usher in the cashless society, the return of Christ, and eventually the end of the world. Be assured, I did not want to be responsible for helping to usher in the end to the world.

I asked my wife if she had ever used one before, and she said, "No, I would be too embarrassed if I did something wrong." I assume she had heard about the alarms sounding and red lights flashing when you messed up.

Natalie (remember, the first Pope to own a debit card) was now a junior at the University of Alabama. She was home for the weekend, and we made a quick trip to Wal-Mart. After we had found our items to purchase we made our way to the checkout line. Being an astute observer of what is going on around me, I noticed that the regular checkout lines each had approximately four hundred people, and the U-Scan lines were totally empty.

So I said, "Natalie, have you ever used a U-Scan checkout lane?" (That was like asking her if the University of Alabama had ever won a national football championship. Of course the answer was yes!) She said, "Sure, Dad, I use them all the time." Now why was I not surprised? Of course college students have absolutely no fear of developing technology and are eager to give it a try!

Knowing that Natalie was with me, I cautiously made my way to the U-Scan station—looking around to see who might be watching. My heart was pounding because I realized that I would be responsible for helping to bring about the end of the world.

I scanned the items, placed them in the bag, and ran into only one small complication that was quickly corrected by pushing a button. We paid with a debit card—with no complications. Mission accomplished! I left the store looking into the sky wondering if I would see that first bolt of lightning indicating Jesus' return.

All kidding aside, I did leave the store very aware that *I (and our society) was one step closer toward a cashless society.* Again, it was *change or be left behind.*

Where do you find yourself as we transition to a cashless society? Are you thinking your participation will help hasten the end of the world? Kicking, shunning, and rebelling? Eager to understand the truth and benefits of a cashless society? Or maybe you find yourself, like most people, somewhere in between and not really sure what to be thinking, biblically and practically.

Are there valid concerns in a cashless society? Are there really more than one billion debit cards in use worldwide? Have global debit card transactions surpassed global credit card transactions? Are we really headed toward a cashless society? The answer to all five questions is a resounding YES!

Are you concerned about the trends you see developing? Or, have you not even taken the time to notice the changing financial landscape around you?

Do you even care that governments and retail and financial institutions are undergoing major changes worldwide?

Have you thought about how these changes might personally affect you and your family?

financial Alert! Alert! Alert!

As a Christian, you should care and you should be aware, because one day you will wake up, and your government will be announcing we have a new currency: U.S. E-dollars. You will need to turn in your green cash to receive your U.S. E-dollars. And by the way, if you rebel and decide to keep your green cash, it will be worthless. You decide. E-dollars or worthless green dollars?

Trust me on this one! The coming cashless society directly relates to you today and in the future. As a Christian you must *seek to understand and adapt to the changing financial world around you* as long as you are not asked to do anything contrary to God's Word.

As Christians, we should be the ones asking the tough questions and providing the best answers.

The coming cashless society affects you, your spouse, your children, your relatives, your church, your government, your business, your friends, and your neighbors.

No one will remain untouched, and no one will be exempt: presidents and members of Congress, married or single, American or foreigner, young or old, well educated or illiterate, rich or poor—everyone.

The goal of *Cashing It In* is to introduce you, your church, your work associates, and even your neighbors and family members to a topic that will be without doubt the most historic event in economic history: the day the world becomes cashless.

Are you ready for a world without cash? *Change or be left behind!*

CHAPTER 2

The signs

*is there any evidence that we are close
to becoming a cashless society?*

TO BE QUITE HONEST, when I began the research for this
book, I did not know what I would discover. I wondered,
*Are we on the eve of a major change, or is it some twenty-five
or more years away?*

I assumed evidence existed out there that the world
was going cashless, but I had no documentation.

All I had were my opinions and some random
newspaper or magazine articles I had stuffed in a file
folder labeled "The Coming Cashless Society." Reading
through my file, I thought to myself, *I have a lot of work
to do.*

As I sat there staring at my file, I began to write
down some of my thoughts and questions about a
cashless society.

Are people actually writing fewer checks and using
less cash? If so, what does this really mean? What percentage of people are using direct deposit? What percentage of

fast-food restaurants are offering cashless? What percentage of people are e-filing their taxes each year? Is it a minuscule 5 percent, or could it be 85 percent? What about our government? Are they becoming cashless? Is there proof? What about other nations, or is this just an American thing? How does the younger generation feel about going cashless? And finally, do we have the technology to operate a global cashless society?

After I made my initial list, my mind flooded with various thoughts, emotions, expectations, concerns, and what-ifs. I sat at my desk and pondered, *What will I really find?* Will the evidence be convincing or insignificant? Are we on the eve of a cashless society, or are we some twenty-five to fifty years away?

Well, several months and hundreds of hours of research later, I am here to announce that the evidence is not only convincing, but it is indisputable! As I will document, in most areas our society is already in the 40 to 80 percent cashless range.

We are rapidly moving toward a cashless society.

As I told my friend Mike, "Let me make this as clear as I can. The fat lady is warming up! *No, she is not singing yet, but she is definitely warming up!"*

Will everyone agree with my analysis? Maybe not, but most will.

After reading this book, will some view me as a radical religious alarmist? Some possibly will, but only those who do not view the Bible and prophecy in the same way that I do.

On the following pages you will find the documentation from my research—a summary of the thousands of pages of documentation I have read, studied, and cataloged.

Every day I receive anywhere from twenty to forty e-mail news alerts on the cashless society: news releases, articles, corporate press releases, and commentary. I can assure you, there is no shortage of information on this topic if you know what you are looking for!

No, I don't plan to provide you with every piece of evidence I dug up and sifted through, but it should be enough information for you to make an intelligent decision concerning our topic.

If you want more research data than this book has to offer, be sure to check out our Web site at **www.foundationsforliving.org** for the most up-to-date information.

Top ten questions to verify the trend to cashless

What I presented to my friends, and I plan to present to you, are the **top ten questions** that I needed to have answered to verify that we are rapidly moving toward a cashless society.

When you finish this chapter, I trust you too will agree there is significant evidence that a *cashless society is coming!*

Send me an e-mail and let me know what you think.

Top Ten Questions To Verify the Cashless Trend

Question #1: Are people writing fewer checks and using more debit cards?

The answer to this first question caught my attention when I learned that the number of debit cards in circulation has grown from practically nothing to over one billion cards in less than ten years. I think you would have to agree that this represents significant growth.

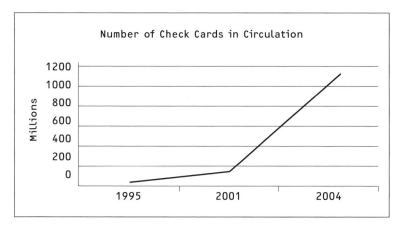

Number of Check Cards in Circulation

The number of debit cards reached one billion in 2003, and it is projected that debit card sales volume will double by 2007.[1]

Next, I learned that the percentage of U.S. households that are using debit cards has grown from about 20 percent in 1995 to over 50 percent in 2003. [2]

I project that 70 to 80 percent of U.S. households will be using a debit card within the next five years.

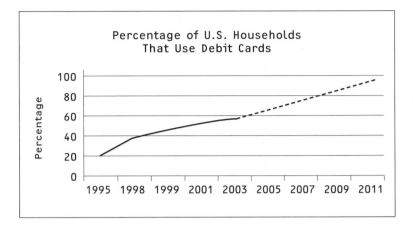

Percentage of U.S. Households That Use Debit Cards

More debit cards mean fewer checks and less necessity for cash.

An April 20, 2004, press release by Visa announced that global debit sales volume for the first time had surpassed credit card sales volume.[3]

Credit sales volume has always been big, but debit sales volume has just become bigger! This is a significant development in the payment industry.

The *Wall Street Journal* reported, "Just four years ago, debit represented only 21 percent of in-store transactions; now one out of three in-store purchases is made with a debit card."[4]

In the coming years we can expect debit card sales volume to continue to exceed and outpace credit card sales volume.

But what about the first part of my question? Are people actually writing fewer checks?

Here is what I found out.

According to the August 2002 *Federal Reserve Bulletin,* the use of paper checks peaked in the mid-1990s and has since been declining at a very measurable rate.[5]

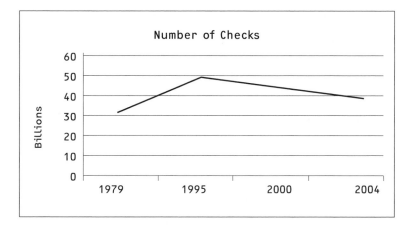

Number of Checks

"Americans wrote a peak of 50 billion checks in the mid-1990s but this year will very likely pen only about 37 billion."[6]

We know that consumers are not spending less, so the only reason for check use to decline would be that other forms of payment (credit, debit, e-commerce) were being used more.

According to *U.S. News & World Report,* the use of checks has been declining at a rate of 4 percent per year and is expected to decline at a greater rate in the future.[7]

"Surveys conducted by the Federal Reserve confirm that electronic payment transactions in the United States have exceeded check payments for the first time. The number of electronic payment transactions totaled 44.5 billion in 2003, while the number of checks paid totaled 36.7 billion."[8]

We can expect the trend of eliminating paper checks to continue and eventually snowball—with only a limited number of check writers holding out until checking is no longer available.

Question #2: What is the percentage of people using internet banking?

What I found was that in less than ten years, the percentage has grown from practically zero to about 40 percent.

In the following chart, the Federal Reserve provided the numbers for 1995 to 2003. Based on my research, I have made projections to 2011.

You don't have to be a prophet to predict that the trend in Internet banking will continue to grow. As reflected in the chart,[9] I believe that 90 percent of people who own a computer will be using some form of Internet banking before 2010.

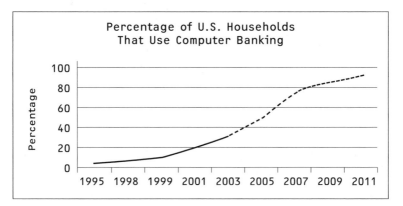

Today, thanks to Internet banking, consumers can access their bank accounts to pay bills, check account balances, transfer funds, set up automatic payments, review bank statements, apply for loans, make investments, order checks, or stop payments on checks. Internet banking is the future.

QUESTION #3: What is the percentage of people using direct deposit?

"Nearly two-thirds of all employees in the United States have their pay deposited directly in a bank account."[10]

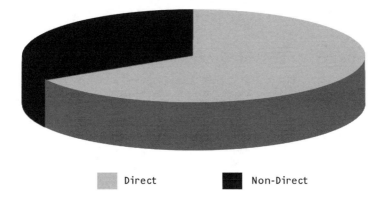

Direct | Non-Direct

Not only are businesses moving toward the use of direct electronic deposits, but also it is very obvious that the government is successfully championing electronic deposits.

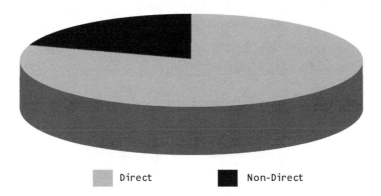

Direct | Non-Direct

"And more than four-fifths of Social Security recipients have benefits deposited directly into their accounts, thanks in part to the U.S. Department of the Treasury's EFT 99 initiative to increase the number of federal payments made electronically."[11]

I would project that within five years, 90 percent of all employee pay will be issued either as direct deposit or as paycards (a type of debit card), and within ten years we will reach 100 percent or be very close to it!

About 10 million U.S. households do not have a bank account. For this group of people, companies are beginning to issue paycards as opposed to paychecks. It is estimated "that 25 percent of all households without bank accounts will be using prepaid cards by next year, up from 8.5 percent in 2003."[12]

Removing the paper paycheck from our society is a major step toward people understanding and becoming comfortable with electronic transfers and cashless transactions!

QUESTION #4: What is the percentage of taxpayers that file their taxes electronically?

Here is what I found by visiting the United States Internal Revenue Service (IRS) Web site (www.irs.gov). In 2004 the IRS received about 128 million individual tax returns—with 61 million, or almost 50 percent, being electronic.

In 1985, filing your tax return electronically was not even an option. Now, twenty years later, approximately 50 percent of all tax returns are filed electronically, and the trend is rapidly increasing!

It was only in 1986 that the Internal Revenue Service began offering e-filing for refund-only individual tax returns. Approximately twenty-five thousand electronic returns were received that year. In 1994 the IRS received 14 million electronic returns and, ten years later in 2004, over 61 million electronic returns.[13]

I just received an IRS Newswire announcing e-filing is running at record pace. "Out of 47 million tax returns filed through Feb. 25, [2005] 74 percent of them were e-filed—up from 69 percent the previous year. While this percentage traditionally declines as April 15 approaches, the IRS expects for the first time to have more than half of all individual tax returns filed electronically. The IRS is also seeing record numbers of people using direct deposit for their refunds. . . . So far this year, three out of four taxpayers receiving refunds have used direct deposit."[14]

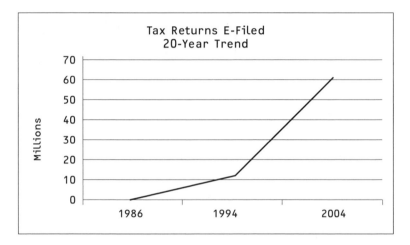

The IRS, beginning in 2006, is requiring that certain large corporations and tax-exempt organizations electronically file their income tax returns. They also strongly encourage all taxpayers to adopt electronic filing.[15]

I project that the U.S. government will require all tax returns to be filed electronically sometime before 2014. Yes, look for a required 100 percent participation rate.

QUESTION #5: what percentage of fast-food restaurants is offering cashless payment options?

At the end of 2004, the percentage of fast-food restaurants accepting some form of cashless payments was: Wendy's

THE SIGNS

at 95 percent; Burger King at 50 percent; McDonald's at 59 percent; Taco Bell at 51 percent; and Jack in the Box at 90 percent.[16]

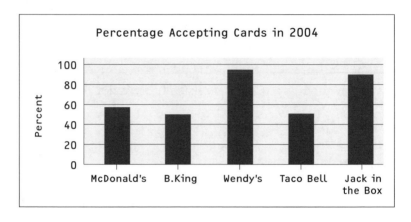

A significant change has taken place over the last two years. Fast-food restaurants that for years refused to accept card payments for meals because of the time involved have abruptly changed their position. Why?

Four reasons:

- Transaction time has been slashed.
- People spend up to 35 percent more when paying cashless.
- The world is going cashless.
- Cashless eliminates employee error at the cash register.

So the decision was simple. They could ignore the new profit potential, ignore the trends, and ignore that customers are looking for cashless payments—or simply be left behind and lose sales to establishments offering cashless payment.

CASE IN POINT: MCDONALD'S

As shown by the following chart, the number of McDonald's restaurants accepting some form of cashless payments has grown from an insignificant number in 2002 to approximately eight thousand in 2004, and cashless options are expected to be available in all thirteen thousand five hundred U.S. restaurants by the end of 2005.

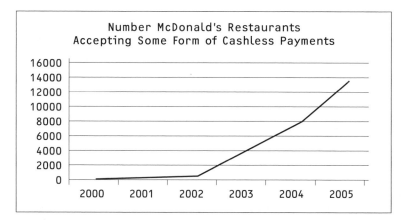

By 2006 virtually all major fast-food restaurant chains (McDonald's, Wendy's, Burger King, and Taco Bell) will be offering cashless payment options.

It has been my conviction for years that when fast-food restaurants begin offering cashless, it's a done deal. Well, fast food is offering cashless!

QUESTION #6: How does the younger generation feel about a cashless society?

Here is what I discovered.

Generation Y, the second largest generation in U.S. history—an estimated 60 million people—is finishing high school and college and moving into the workforce.

These are the future consumers who know only a

world filled with ATMs, e-mail, credit and debit cards, U-Scan stations in stores, cell phones, and making purchases using shopping carts on the Internet. "They're coming to expect that their payment cards will offer things paper money and even checks can't provide—advantages like: security protection, dispute resolution, rewards...and more."[17]

We can expect the older generations to actively resist the coming cashless society, while the younger generation expects nothing but a cashless society. What Generation Y knows is debit cards, the Internet, and little cash. Becoming cashless is a no-brainer for Generation Y.

QUESTION #7: what is the u.s. government doing in the area of cashless?

Here is my logic in needing to know the answer to this question: If the government is not involved and supportive, it is not going to happen! If they are big promoters, it is going to happen!

Actually, what I found was amazing. I had no idea that our government had become so "pro-cashless." They are making policy changes in every department.

Here are a few examples of the changes taking place.

CASHLESS MILITARY BASES
The Treasury is replacing coin and currency in circulation on military bases and ships worldwide with stored-value cards.[18]

ELECTRONIC SAVING BONDS
"In addition, the Treasury is considering a plan to stop issuing paper savings bond certificates and to instead

issue electronic savings bonds. Consumers would purchase the savings bonds online instead of at financial institutions, and the bonds would be stored electronically, as Treasury bills, notes, and bonds are currently."[19]

CHILD-SUPPORT AND UNEMPLOYMENT PAYMENTS

The government now issues child support and unemployment payments through electronic cards.

LOCAL, STATE, AND FEDERAL AGENCIES

It is predicted that most local, state, and federal agencies will be using electronic payments in the next few years.

CHECK CLEARING ACT

The Check Clearing for the 21st Century Act went into effect on October 28, 2004. This new law allows banks to replace paper checks they receive with an electronic version of the check called an IRD (image replacement document). The Check 21 Act represents another proactive move on the part of the U.S. government to move away from paper processing to electronic processing. This act will also save banks millions of dollars in the transportation and processing of paper checks.

I am convinced the U.S. government is leading the way toward a cashless society and, in my opinion, will become the first institution to go 100 percent cashless.

Question #8: Are more people using plastic for smaller, frequent purchases?

Let me explain my logic as I researched this question. If people are continuing to use plastic only for the big purchases, we have a long way to go before becoming cashless. Because in a cashless society, everybody will need to feel comfortable buying a soft drink with plastic or waving his or her hand in front of the drink machine so it can read the implanted chip.

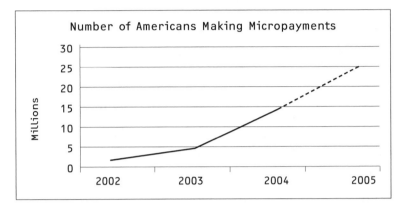

Here is what I found in seeking to answer that question. Over the last couple of years, micropayments (less than five dollars) using the Internet and mobile devices are finally on the radar screen. In 2003, 4 million consumers made micropayments. In 2004 that number rose to over 14 million. This is an increase of 350 percent in just one year. I personally estimate this number could reach up to 25 million in 2005. In addition, revenues from micropayments are expected to increase at a compound annual growth rate of 23 percent.[20]

A recent report documented that most consumers using vending machines favor cashless transactions.[21] *There is the answer I was looking for!* People have become very comfortable buying even a drink with a cashless transaction.

For years, purchases using plastic have been reserved for items that cost over five dollars. However, with the use of debit and smart gift cards, that is all changing.

In a few years, the norm will be for everyone to pay for everything using an electronic transaction—plastic or contactless (a card that needs only to be moved close to, and not actually touch, a card reader).

QUESTION #9: is the cashless trend an American thing? or is the world going cashless?

The answer to this question took a considerable amount of time, but I was able to find enough data to convince me that the world is going cashless!

As you will see, my research confirmed that cashless, electronic, and contactless payments are not just developing in the United States but around the world. Space would not allow me to list everything being reported globally. However, here is a small sampling of reports coming out of other nations.

SOUTH AFRICA

"One of our core business strategies in South Africa is to continue to focus on expanding Visa debit cards to the substantial unbanked population, accelerate our progress to a cashless society, as well as to increase consumer awareness and encourage greater payment-card usage" (Chris Winter, Visa CEMEA's [Central and Eastern Europe, Middle East, and Africa] general manager and senior vice-president for sub-Saharan Africa).[22]

MALAYSIA

A new chip-based card in Malaysia is replacing over 11 million ATM cards. This is part of the government's plan to develop a national electronic banking system and a cashless society. The new cards will not only have ATM options, but also include e-Debit and e-Purse applications.

e-Debit will allow for cashless payments for goods and services.

e-Purse will allow the cardholder to store "electronic cash" that can be used for low-value purchases—much like a gift card.

Visa is testing its Visa Wave contactless card at over one hundred fifty merchant locations.

JORDAN
Credit cards are spreading rapidly in Jordan. It was only in the early 1990s that Visa International began developing the market. Now more than five hundred thousand people in Jordan are using the Visa card.

CANADA
In Canada the taxi industry is moving cashless. This is significant, because the taxi industry in every city around the world is known for being a cash-transaction industry! If they are beginning to offer cashless options, this is a big deal!

FRANCE
The move in France toward a cashless society is full steam ahead. In 2001, the Moneo "smart card" was introduced that allows consumers to store up to one hundred euro (approximately one hundred dollars). The goal in France is to dispense with pocket change and improve the speed for small transactions. Users can upload more euros from their bank accounts at teller machines.

BRITAIN

In Britain, consumers will spend more using debit and credit cards than cash this year. Eighty-two percent of adults own debit cards in Britain. And the use of debit cards will account for two-thirds of plastic transactions in that nation.

JAPAN

Japan is leading the way in the development of paying for items using mobile phone technology. Some are already saying that wallets may soon become a thing of the past in Japan.

INDIA

Visa India is making plans for businesses to begin using payroll cards (paycards). The prepaid payroll cards can be used to make purchases or withdraw cash from an ATM. Credit and debit card use in India is also growing.

SOUTH KOREA

Using cell phones for financial transactions is booming. In 2004 approximately six hundred thousand South Koreans were using their cell phones to complete banking transactions. Every month, three hundred thousand South Koreans are buying new cell phones that have a special slot where banking data can be added.

AUSTRALIA, TAIWAN, THAILAND

Use of credit and debit cards is growing rapidly.

KUWAIT

Kuwait was the first country in the Middle East to launch a cell-phone payment system.

RUSSIA

The Moscow Social Card combines identity, cash access, health care, and public transit into one card. Some sixty agencies are delivering benefits to over 2.5 million residents.

GLOBALLY

Practically in every nation, credit cards are now used and accepted. Major credit card companies see the potential for growth and therefore more profits in many countries around the world.

We should expect more news from every nation about credit and debit card use rising. We should also expect increased use worldwide of smart cards containing small computer chips that provide personal and financial data.

In addition, there will come a day when every person on the face of the earth will have a global financial account number. How can I say this? For Revelation 13 to become a reality one day, there appears no other option. No one will have the ability to buy or sell unless they have the mark of the Beast. The mark of the Beast will require some type of individual numbering system. I'll discuss this prophetic connection in more detail in chapter 9.

Finally, I had to ask one of the most important questions.

QUESTION #10: Do we have a global financial network that is already established and can handle a cashless society?

The answer: We have the ability and the computer power to process transactions on a global scale.

"In the 1970s, the pioneers at Visa hoped we would find a way to process ten transactions a second. Just thirty years later, we're looking to a future where we'll process more than ten thousand transactions a second. That's progress," according to the president of Visa USA.[23]

Plans are already being made to develop a **worldwide wireless network.** Intel, which controls 82.9 percent of the market worldwide for PC microprocessors, has in its sights the development of a wireless infrastructure worldwide.

Intel's Chief Technology Officer and Senior Vice President Pat Gelsinger said, "Over the next decade, the majority of the world will communicate wirelessly."[24] Gelsinger also said, "Wireless communication will become truly ubiquitous."[25]

In case you are wondering, *Webster's* defines ubiquitous as: "present, or seeming to be present, everywhere at the same time; omnipresent." What does this mean to you and me?

WHAT IS A HOT SPOT?

Today we have "hot spots" for wireless communication in relatively few places. Hot spots are areas within public or private venues (homes, dorm rooms, airports, hotels, stores, coffee shops, libraries, parks, government buildings, and schools) where individuals can gain high-speed access to the Internet using wireless technology.

In the future the entire world will be a hot spot.

Not only does this mean we will be able to connect to the Internet anywhere in the world, but these technological developments will serve as the infrastructure for instant transfer of funds to and from anywhere in the world.

Let's not pass over this potential development too quickly. This is very significant for a global cashless society. This global hot-spot development will serve as the technology for you and me to process a transaction from literally anywhere in the world. We could be standing on the observation deck at Niagara Falls, on the side of the road in a souvenir shop, or in the backwoods of Africa and be able to make a financial transaction!

The global hot-spot technology is not in operation today but will be a reality in the future.

Does a cashless society mean we will have to operate on one currency worldwide?

A cashless society does not necessarily mean that we will have to operate on one currency worldwide. We already have the technology to support multiple currencies worldwide.

Each nation can retain its own currency. Travelers already have the ability to make cashless purchases, with the currency conversions made automatically by the card company following the transactions. Point-of-sale terminals already show the cost in two or more currencies.

Summary

My research has verified my assumption that we are not in the 5 or 10 percent cashless participation range, but in the 40 to 80 percent cashless participation range. Let's have a quick review:

- Fewer checks are being written each year.
- More debit cards are being used each year.

- Traditionally "cash only" establishments like fast-food restaurants will all be accepting cashless options before 2006.
- The use of Internet banking is up each year.
- The use of direct deposit is up each year.
- E-filing (electronic filing) of tax returns is up each year.
- The government is moving more toward cashless each year.
- Generation Y is practically cashless already.
- Micropayments are substantially up each year.
- The world is trending cashless.
- The global financial network is in place.

Whether you like it, agree with it, or hate it, a cashless society is on the way. But, as some of my friends asked me at this point, "What is it that makes this topic so controversial?"

I think the answer to that question can be summed up in one word: **"Uncertainty!"** That means concerns—about the unknown, about security, and about being forced to change. A cashless society involves all these things plus much more!

As my friends already understood, this topic is raging with controversial issues.

In the next two chapters, we will look at the controversial aspects or, as some might say, the *"darker side"* of a cashless society:

- RFID tags everywhere
- Loss of privacy

- Implantable computer chips
- Personal locators
- Persecution

Before you turn the page, why don't you make your way to the kitchen and get a fresh cup of coffee or a big bowl of ice cream. If you have to go out for your coffee or ice cream—don't forget to take your debit card!

If you have your cup of coffee or big bowl of ice cream, turn the page and travel with me into the land of "what-ifs" and the territory of "unknowns."

[1] "Visa Global Debit Card Sales Volume Surpasses Credit," April 20, 2004, http://usa.visa.com/personal/newsroom/press_releases/nr209.html?it=search.

[2] "U.S. Consumers and Electronic Banking, 1995-2003," *Federal Reserve Bulletin* (Winter 2004): 6.

[3] "Visa Global Debit Card Sales Volume Surpasses Credit," April 20, 2004. http://usa.visa.com/personal/newsroom/press_releases/nr209.html?it=search.

[4] Robin Sidel, "Cash? What's Cash?" the *Wall Street Journal,* January 31, 2005, R3.

[5] "The Use of Checks and Other Noncash Payment Instruments in the United States," *Federal Reserve Bulletin* (August 2002): 360.

[6] Kim Clark, "Marked For Extinction," *U.S. News and World Report,* September 20, 2004, 38.

[7] Ibid.

[8] Federal Reserve Board Press Release, 12/6/04. http://www.federalreserve.gov/boarddocs/press/other/2004/20041206.

[9] "U.S. Consumers and Electronic Banking, 1995-2003," *Federal Reserve Bulletin* (Winter 2004).

[10] Ibid.

[11] Ibid.

[12] Sidel, "Cash? What's Cash?" the *Wall Street Journal*.

[13] http://www.irs.gov/pub/irs-soi/03ifssct/.txt.

[14] IRS Newswire, 3/2/05, IR-2005-21.

[15] IRS Newswire, 1/11/05, IR-2005-8.

[16] "McDonald's Joins Pay-with-Plastic Trend," *USA Today*, July 23, 2004, 1b.

[17] Carl Pascarella, Visa USA President and CEO (Keynote Address, American Bankers Association Bank Card Conference, Dallas, TX, September 22, 2003).

[18] "U.S. Consumers and Electronic Banking, 1995–2003," *Federal Reserve Bulletin* (Winter 2004): 16.

[19] Ibid.

[20] http://www.clickz.com/stats/markets/retailing/article.php/3419901.

[21] 11/17/2004, http://www.prnewswire.com.

[22] http://www.mg.co.za/Content/13.asp?cg=BreakingNews-Business&ao=122504.

[23] Pascarella (Keynote Address).

[24] http://www.intel.com/pressroom/archive/releases/20030918corp.htm.

[25] Ibid.

CHAPTER 3

The Technology Controversy

What is RFID?

TALK RADIO IS ONE OF MY FAVORITE ACTIVITIES. I just love to take part in programs when I can dialogue with the host or caller. What an incredible opportunity for ministry—the potential for thousands, if not hundreds of thousands or millions, of people listening in on the conversation!

Before I even do my first radio program on *Cashing It In,* I can already see how this controversial topic might play out on the air.

I am confident the first thing the host will want to talk about is *whether a cashless society is a sign the world is about to end.* Some will ask in a kidding or sarcastic way, while others will be very serious.

In answering their question, is this the end of the world? of course, I will say yes and advise everyone to purchase a steel helmet and start running for the hills... Just kidding!

All joking aside, after the host and I have discussed how a cashless society ties in with end times (see chapter 9), I expect that every available telephone line will be taken. I can imagine the first call going something like this:

Caller: "Hi, Ethan. This is such an interesting topic you are talking about. I had never really thought much about a cashless society until today. Wow, you have really opened my eyes and gotten my attention."

Ethan: "That's encouraging to hear. It is a very interesting topic, and I am glad you are finding it helpful. How can I help you today?"

Caller: "Well, Ethan, from a biblical perspective, please tell me, what should I be the most concerned about in a cashless society? Or is there anything to be concerned about?"

Ethan: "That is a great question. Actually there are a number of things we need to be aware of. Let me begin with what I believe to be the most important: *how a cashless society will affect your privacy.*"

Caller: "Oh, really? How is a cashless society related to my privacy?"

Ethan: "Let me explain … "

To describe how a cashless society relates to my privacy, I will need to answer this question in *two parts.* I will cover the first aspect, key technologies, in this chapter and continue the discussion in the next chapter on how applying these technologies can invade our privacy.

The first question we all need to be asking is:

Do you want the government or some institution to have the potential to view every financial transaction you make, track every store or restaurant you have visited, and be able to know your exact location?

To understand how all of this could even be possible, you must first understand the basics of a device already being used: a Radio Frequency Identification tag (RFID).

CONTROVERSIAL ISSUE #1: RFID

What are Radio Frequency Identification tags, and how do they relate to a cashless society?

Remember when the UPC (Universal Product Code) was first introduced? Some thought the UPC was the mark of the Beast (Revelation 13) and would become the mark that everyone would be receiving on his or her forehead or right hand. Numerous best-selling books and articles were written about it.

Well, it looks like everyone got all worked up over nothing. The infamous UPC mark will soon fade into history if the developers and promoters of RFID technology have anything to say about it. I might add that major retailers are really the ones who will ultimately determine the success or failure of RFID technology.

RFID uses a tiny computer chip with an antenna that can receive electromagnetic energy beamed at it from a reader device. Once the chip picks up the signal, it sends back to the receiver its unique identification number or other information requested—allowing the item or person with RFID chip to be specifically identified.

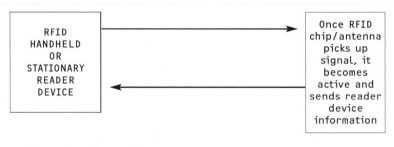

RFID HANDHELD OR STATIONARY READER DEVICE

Once RFID chip/antenna picks up signal, it becomes active and sends reader device information

The technology for RFID goes back to World War II when ground troops could beam radio signals to an aircraft's transponder to help reduce friendly fire. Therefore, the concept has really been in development for many years.

PASSIVE AND ACTIVE TAGS

There are passive and active RFID tags. Active tags have a battery, which broadcasts a signal to a reader. Passive tags do not have a battery and become activated only when they receive a signal from a reader. Most RFID tags being used today are passive.

READ-WRITE TAGS

Some tags are read-only, while other tags are read-write. The read-only tags can store only the data that has been put on the tags from a manufacturer. The read-write tags come with information from a manufacturer, but additional information can be added in warehouses or when sold. For example, when an item is sold, the store could write on the RFID tag exactly when and where the item was purchased. It is also possible that the store could write on the tag who purchased the item.

READING DISTANCE

Low frequency readers can read passive tags approximately one foot away or less. High frequency readers can read passive tags ten to twenty feet away. Readers communicating with active tags (with batteries) can read in ranges of three hundred feet or more.

CURRENT COMMON APPLICATIONS
OF RFID TECHNOLOGY:

- Identify and track livestock
- Identify pets (More than 25 million pets and live-stock have been implanted with RFID.)
- Identify and track people (See section in next chapter on implantable VeriChips.)
- Track objects or assets
- Control inventory in warehouses or store shelves
- Locate and track library books
- Security and ID cards
- Track and identify luggage
- Locate lost golf balls (makers of golf balls don't like this one!)
- Cashless payments and transactions
- Prevent items from being stolen (An alarm goes off.)

Let's take a more detailed look at some of these applications listed above. This is not some sci-fi technology. My research has revealed that this technology is available or even actually being used in the following ways today:

TRACKING SCHOOL CHILDREN
Some schools are now tracking the location of students. In Osaka, Japan, all the school children have been given an RFID tag that can be attached to their clothing. When the kids enter or leave the school, the time and location will be sent home by e-mail.

DOORS AND LOCKS

RFID could replace door keys and locks. In the future, all you might need to do would be wave your watch or arm to open a door lock at your home or office.

AMUSEMENT PARKS

Several amusement parks are now using RFID watchlike devices that children and family members can wear during their visit to the park. Should a child become lost, parents can go to one of seven kiosks and wave their Star Watch over a reader, and a screen will immediately show them the location of every member in their group. Users can also send messages to other group members during their stay. Each Star Watch device rents for five dollars per day. Few groups are renting the Star Watches so far, but one upgrade that might increase use would be allowing groups to put money on their Star Watch accounts so they can buy snacks and merchandise simply by scanning their watch. Sounds like a cashless society amusement park to me.

MEDICAL USE

RFID tags are being tested in hospitals for patient identi- fication, and to access a wireless database to find out patient information, order lab tests, make notes, or update medical information.

AIRPORTS

One of the major airlines is testing RFID baggage tags for security purposes and for finding lost luggage. Hong Kong International Airport plans to use RFID tags to monitor luggage and increase airport security.

HELPING THE BLIND
Japan is reportedly working on RFID readers in sidewalks to help blind people.

PRISONS
Select prisons in California, Michigan, and Ohio are using wristwatch-size transmitters to track the locations of all prisoners. In addition, guards wear the technology on their belts so they can be tracked for security.

INVENTORY MONITORING
Some stores are testing RFID readers placed beneath shelves to monitor product inventory in real time. When a consumer removes an item from the shelf and places it in his or her shopping cart, the inventory count is reduced immediately. Once the shelf inventory reaches a specified number, the warehouse is alerted to restock the specific item. Why have five cases sitting in the warehouse until 11 p.m. when the shelf is empty at 9 a.m.? Out-of-stock items cost supermarkets an estimated $6 billion in lost sales each year.[1]

INDIVIDUAL PRODUCT TAGS
Some retailers already stock individual items, like printers and scanners, with RFID tags. Each item has a sticker indicating that it contains an RFID tag. This tag is provided because of the growing controversy over the use of RFID tags and invasion-of-privacy issues.

A well-known clothing store has tested placing tags on jeans at the factory. Once the jeans are purchased, the cash register writes onto the tags indicating when and where they were purchased. This could prove to be a valuable tool to combat shoplifting.

RFID PAYMENT CHIP
In 2003, according to MasterCard's Web site (www.mastercard.com) MasterCard launched PayPass, a contactless card. They also began working with Nokia to test using PayPass in mobile phones.

EUROS
The European Union is considering placing a tiny RFID chip in every paper euro note, providing both counterfeiting protection and the ability to give each bill a unique serial number.[2]

GAMBLING CHIPS
Chipco is developing RFID chips to be used in casinos.

ANTITHEFT
RFID tags are already being used to prevent theft of expensive items like computers, software, and music CDs. Have you ever paid for an item and walked out the door, only to hear an alarm go off? I surely have. What was the problem? An RFID tag had not been removed or deactivated. Proponents of RFID want to take this to a whole new level! Not only will RFID tags be used for expensive items, but for literally every item in the store: toothbrushes, shoe polish, batteries, and even toilet paper.

PROMOTIONAL POTENTIAL
What if you picked up a movie from the shelf and a video player began playing action clips from the movie you are holding in your hand? Cool. Or how about if you hold a dress up near an RFID monitor and you immediately see

models wearing the exact dress in the color you are holding and in the five different colors available?

HOSPITALS

Some hospitals are using RFID bracelets to tag newborns immediately after birth.

CONTACTLESS PAYMENT DEVICES

Mobil Speedpass and E-ZPass toll road devices both use RFID technology. When asked how many people have heard of Speedpass or E-ZPass, about 50 percent of those surveyed said they have either used them or heard about them.

WHY WILL RFID TECHNOLOGY BE USED IN THE FUTURE?

Current RFID technology has been around since at least the 1970s. But, due to the per-tag expense, it has been impractical to use it for *individual product* identification. However, some of the largest retail stores are beginning to require that manufacturers who ship to them have RFID tags on the pallets or cases.

Let's take Wal-Mart, for example. When Wal-Mart speaks, manufacturers listen! Wal-Mart mandated that their top one hundred suppliers begin using RFID tags on cases of items ordered by 2005.[3] On April 30, 2004, the Dallas-Fort Worth distribution center began receiving cases and pallets of products marked with RFID tags— a major milestone in the RFID industry.

The Pentagon also requires its top suppliers to use RFID tags.

Target and Albertson's have also issued similar mandates following Wal-Mart's lead.

It is very interesting to note that over twenty years ago, it was Wal-Mart that mandated that suppliers begin using bar codes (UPC) on every product. They almost single-handedly made the bar code ubiquitous.[4] It looks like Wal-Mart will once again be the key player who will make RFID ubiquitous.

what is the difference in UPC and RFID?

RFID differs from the UPC bar code in the following ways:

UPC Bar Code	RFID	Contrast
All bar codes on cans of soft drinks of the same brand and flavor are the same.	Each individual soft drink can would have a unique ID number.	General code versus a very specific unique ID code.
Must be scanned, a very public act. Line-of-sight technology. Bar code must be visible to be read.	If within range, an RFID tag can be read by a reader without your even knowing it.	Line-of-sight reader compared to having a tag within a specific range to be read.
Must be printed on surface.	RFID tag can actually be hidden. Tag can be between layers of cardboard, sewn in clothes labels, and molded inside plastic or rubber.	Visible versus hidden.

HOW AWARE ARE CONSUMERS ABOUT RFID TECHNOLOGY?

Only 23 percent of consumers have heard of RFID technology.[5] Because of the growing RFID controversy and publicity, I project that within three years this number will increase to at least 90 percent.

WHAT ARE THE SECURITY AND INVASION-OF-PRIVACY CONCERNS?

Between 40 and 50 percent of one thousand consumers expect RFID technology to create greater personal privacy issues than cell phones, ATMs, or credit and debit cards have.[6]

SINGLE GLOBAL TECHNOLOGY

"Kevin Ashton, former executive director of a joint corporate and academic RFID research center at the Massachusetts Institute of Technology, said in a promotional video that the organization's mission was to 'create a single global technology that will enable computers to identify an object, anywhere, automatically,' " according to the *Washington Post.*[7]

WHAT INFORMATION CAN BE CONTAINED IN THE RFID CHIP?

- Item name
- Color
- Weight
- Price
- Sales price
- Date produced
- Where produced
- Inspected by
- Date shipped
- Date received
- Date put on shelves

- Date sold
- PLUS just about anything else anyone wants to include!

Remember, data can be added to read-write chips as they progress from the manufacturer to the retailer to the consumer.

A look into the future

Imagine if every specific product in your home had an RFID tag, and if you had an RFID reader in your home that could cover every room in your house.
This is what you would be able to do:

- By simply looking at your computer screen, you could see where every lost shoe is located in your house.
- You could see how many bottles of shampoo you have remaining on the shelf.
- You could be informed if you have any products that have been recalled and exactly where they are located.
- You could have an instant inventory of every item in real time!
- You would have access to information about when you purchased that computer printer sitting in your office and if it is still under warranty.

I think you get the picture. Make no mistake! RFID is a big issue and a growing issue! In addition to RFID, another technology issue should concern everyone.

CONTROVERSIAL ISSUE #2:
Dependency on Computers

Obviously, a cashless society will be 100 percent dependent on the use of computers. Without computers in operation, you can have no cashless transactions, because all cashless transactions are electronic.

Today, when a computer crashes, we do have the option to use cash or write a paper check to complete the transaction.

Let's list the possible problems with a system that is completely computer dependent.

1. It's a fact! Computers do stop working. I have yet to purchase a computer that has operated with perfection.

2. Viruses can infect computers and create major problems. In all our inventions, we have yet to create software that protects our computers 100 percent.

3. You know that thousands of computer hackers will be attempting to shut the system down—for evil reasons or just to see if they can do it!

4. We must acknowledge that there will be terrorist attacks on the cashless system. What better way to disrupt the lives of billions of people around the world?

In my opinion, this issue is *titanic in importance.* We must have adequate backup systems and security firewalls in place. The global use of computers in buying and selling is a perfect fit for Revelation 13 and biblical prophecy.

Now for a final thought

Technology in itself is not evil, but evil men can use technology for harm.

Consider this: If given the opportunity, do you think Hitler, Stalin, Mao, Hussein, and Bin Laden would have used a cashless society to control and punish their enemies? Of course they would! Just rewind history for a short sixty years when Hitler's goal was to exterminate the Jews. Think how Hitler could and would have used a cashless system for the sake of national security! How could Hitler have used technology for evil? He could have immediately identified the list of people who were financially supporting the Jewish synagogue or had supported political groups who were opposing his regime! Boom! A complete list of names, addresses, and financial data. *And as we will learn in the next chapter, if they had been implanted with a computer chip, he would be able to know their exact location!*

Ponder what this could mean for believers who are finding themselves in a world rapidly moving toward a zero tolerance for Christians.

In the next chapter we will take a closer look at how RFID technology, computers, implantable computer chips, personal tracking devices, global positioning satellites, *and* biometrics can be used both for good and to invade your privacy.

[1] *USA Today,* October 7, 2003.

[2] www.msnbc.msn.com/id/306887/site/newsweek.

[3] *Fortune,* 148, November 10, 2003: 46.

[4] Ibid.

[5] http://h71028.www/7.hp.com/enterprise/cache/20135-0-0-225-121.aspx.

[6] Ibid.

[7] Jonathan Krim, "Embedding Their Hopes in RFID," the *Washington Post,* June 23, 2004: E1.

CHAPTER 4

The Privacy controversy

should I be concerned about anything?

NOW THAT WE KNOW SOMETHING of what RFID technology is and how it works, let's take a closer look at a deeper issue.

HOW CAN RFID AND A CASHLESS SOCIETY BE USED TO INVADE MY PRIVACY?

Let me summarize some of the pros and cons of tracking your every financial transaction and move.

Promoters of the cashless society say:

- A cashless society will make life easier and simpler.
- No one is tracking where you shop, where you visit, and what you do.
- No one is tracking every detail of your financial transactions.
- No one wants to know where you have been.
- No one wants to know about your financial transactions.

- If you are not doing anything wrong, you have no need to be concerned.

- If you are doing something wrong, we need to have the ability to stop you.

Privacy proponents would say (and I would agree with most of their points):

- The potential to track where we shop and what we do is real.

- The potential to monitor every financial transaction is real.

- The potential for this information to be used by some evil person or evil institution is real.

- The potential for good people to be hurt is real.

- The best thing to do is not allow invasion of privacy to happen.

Did you know that 41 percent of Americans oppose some type of a national identification system?[1] I believe that in the coming cashless society, we will have some form of a national identification system, and every transaction will be recorded and could be monitored.

Real-Life Situations

Now let's look at more ways the RFID technology we discussed in the last chapter can be used in real-life situations.

Imagine walking into a store, and an RFID tag sewn in the label of your jacket tells the reader at the entrance of the store when and where you purchased the jacket and how much you paid for it—or if you even purchased it at all! If the RFID tag in your jacket does not contain any "sales" information, you could become an immediate suspect for shoplifting.

For example, if every item of clothing has an imbedded RFID tag, a store could determine what brand or price range of clothing is the most common for their regular customers. Then within weeks, they could begin offering that brand or price range of clothing—because that is what their customers are buying and wearing! Some could view this as a positive, while others could view this as an invasion of privacy rights.

If we all have a personal RFID tag (in our wallet, on our watch, or implanted under our skin) when we enter a store, we could immediately be identified. It is possible that as you walk into a store, your name could flash on a computer screen and a greeter could welcome you by name. If you are a regular customer, you might be immediately offered a 20-percent-off coupon for everything you purchase that day. Once again, this could be viewed as a positive or negative development—positive in the sense that you are offered discounts, negative if this offer will cause you to spend more than you had planned.

The greatest concern of privacy watch groups involves the potential to track your every move: which stores you visit, which movies you watched, when you visited the bank, and where you purchased your gas. Every move, every purchase, every aspect of your life could be recorded and monitored.

Some **solutions** include not having an RFID computer chip permanently attached to or in our body. Or we must have the ability to turn off the RFID tag as we walk in and around the store.

Most RFID industry leaders estimate that individual products with read-write tags will begin to be used within ten years. Current RFID tag price: thirty-five cents per tag for volume orders, to as much as seventy cents.[2] The goal for massive quantities of individual RFID tags is two to five cents.

Look for invasion-of-privacy issues to become the main focus with RFID technology. The battle has just begun, and the issues are far from being resolved! I also believe that Congress will eventually have to become involved in regulating the use of RFID tags.

The next question I think we should be asking is: **should I consider having an implantable computer chip that stores financial and health information, and has the ability to reveal my location anywhere on the earth?**

CONTROVERSIAL ISSUE #3:
implantable computer chips

The technology is not fully developed but is in process. One company is making most of the news in this area. Applied Digital Solutions is the parent company for makers of the VeriChip™ and Digital Angel®.

WHAT IS THE VERICHIP?
VeriChip is a small device containing a computer chip and radio frequency identification (RFID) technology that can be inserted under your skin using a syringe. Each chip can contain

Used with permission.

unique personal, financial, and medical information. The chip can also be updated once implanted.

An enlarged picture of a VeriChip appears on the previous page. The promotions say that the VeriChip is about the size of a grain of rice.

As of 2004, seven thousand VeriChips have been sold. About one thousand have been implanted.[3] The first person to receive the implanted chip was Dr. Richard Seelig, a New Jersey surgeon, on September 16, 2001. Seelig serves as a medical consultant for Applied Digital. Dr. Seelig said he was motivated to implant the VeriChip in his body after seeing firefighters on September 11, 2001 writing their names and Social Security numbers on their forearms with a magic marker.

Another historic moment took place on May 10, 2002. On national television, Jeffrey and Leslie Jacobs and their son Derek received implanted VeriChips on NBC's *Today* show—as the headlines read, the first family to "get chipped."

After years of trying to receive approval, Applied Digital Solutions was cleared by the U.S. Food and Drug Administration on October 14, 2004, to use the VeriChip for medical uses. According to a press release by Applied Digital, the "VeriChip is a subdermal RFID device that can be used in a variety of security, financial, emergency identification and other applications."[4]

Note the potential uses: security, financial, and identification!

WHAT INFORMATION IS ACTUALLY CONTAINED IN THE CHIP?

Currently the VeriChip contains only a person's name and a unique identification number. Once the VeriChip is scanned with a reader, the name and number appear on a computer screen. The number is then entered into what the manufacturer calls a "secure" computer database to retrieve personal information.

The "secure" computer database could include the following:

- Name
- Birth date
- Address
- Social Security number
- Insurance information
- Employer
- Basic medical information
- Advanced medical information such as recent X-rays
- Medicines you are currently taking
- Medicines to which you are allergic
- Contact information—phone numbers, etc.
- Financial information
- PLUS much more

WHAT ARE THE POTENTIAL FUTURE BENEFITS OF BEING "CHIPPED"?

Listed below are just a few of the potential future benefits of having a RFID computer chip—either implanted under your skin or on a card, bracelet, or necklace:

- No more having to remember passwords
- No more remembering Social Security numbers
- Open secured doors just by approaching

- Walk out of grocery stores without having to stop and pay
- Chip-friendly homes that could do the following:

  - ◆ Open doors when you approach
  - ◆ Customize temperatures when you walk into a room
  - ◆ Begin playing your favorite music

- Identify Alzheimer's patients
- Identify amnesiac patients
- Identify babies in hospitals
- Identify hospital patients
- Identify accident victims
- Identify personnel allowed to enter secure offices or sites
- Locating people
- Locating soldiers in times of war

People have been implanting various items into their bodies for years, so what makes this one any different? For example we have implanted ...

- Pacemakers for the heart
- Silicone for the breast
- Hearing aids for the ear
- Rods and screws for broken bones
- New knees or hips
- Metal plates in the head

First let me note that all the items listed above, with the exception of breast implants, are for medical reasons. In addition, none of those items are programmed to provide and signal any personal data that involves your identification, health, or financial data. Yet that is the intended purpose of the VeriChip.

IS THE IMPLANTABLE COMPUTER CHIP CONTROVERSIAL?

Just read some of these recent newspaper and magazine headlines about the implantable chip, and you decide!

- Injectable Chip Opens Door to Human Bar Code
- Computer Chip Implanted in Humans Could Be Tracking, Info Device
- The Personal Microchip Is Being Touted as the Next-Generation ID Card
- Hype Surrounds First Chip Implant
- Florida Firm Seeks FDA Approval for Human Chip Implants
- Microchips Being Implanted in Humans for Emergencies
- Microchip Located People
- Invisible "Mark of the Beast"?
- Big Brother Gets Under Your Skin
- Microchip Implanted in Mexican Officials

THE RAGING CONTROVERSY

In the previous chapter on RFID, I listed numerous beneficial ways RFID technology is currently being used and could be used in the future. But, even with the numerous present and potential benefits, the controversy continues in two main areas over using RFID in implantable chips:

- Potential invasion of privacy—the Big Brother theory
- Biblical prophecy—is this the mark of the Beast?

The concern is that once an individual is implanted with an RFID VeriChip, the potential for harm becomes widespread—which leads us to our next question:

What are the pros and cons of having an implantable chip or other device that has the ability to provide my exact location at any time?

CONTROVERSIAL ISSUE #4: PERSONAL TRACKING DEVICES

Most of the media hype is over the potential loss of privacy. Do we really want someone or some institution or government agency to have the ability to track our movement?

I can think of two advantages of being tracked: (1) If you are lost, a rescue team would be able to locate you. (2) If you were kidnapped, the police would be able to find you.

Now for the darker side. If you are kidnapped, and the kidnappers know that everyone has an implantable chip, what do you think they would do? Take a knife and cut it out!

In order for anyone to be tracked, the person and the trackers must rely on a Global Positioning System (GPS).

WHAT IS THE GLOBAL POSITIONING SYSTEM, AND HOW DOES IT WORK?

GPS is a group of 28 satellites orbiting the earth. Twenty-four are in operation, with four backups. The orbits are arranged so that at least four satellites are visible from any point on the earth.

Courtesy U.S. Department of Defense

Initial Purpose

GPS was initially developed for military use and is now being used for military and nonmilitary purposes. The fleet of satellites is controlled from Schriever Air Force Base, east of Colorado Springs, Colorado.

How GPS Works

The system works by a GPS receiver determining its position on the earth by a process called triangulation. The receiver on the ground determines its distance from at least three satellites and calculates its location on earth.

It is estimated that at least one hundred thousand receivers are being built and sold each month.

EXAMPLES OF CURRENT USES
OF GPS TECHNOLOGY

- Military operations
- GPS-equipped cell phones transmit your location when you call 911. This becomes even more relevant because the Federal Communications Commission (FCC) has mandated that by the end of 2005 all cell phones must include GPS that pinpoints the location of the cell phone. It's called the "E911" mandate. This is an interesting development in the whole issue of privacy.
- GPS receivers are tracking released prisoners.
- GPS golf carts tell players exactly how far their ball lies from the hole. It is estimated that over eight thousand golf courses will be using the GPS golf system by the end of 2005.
- GPS informs employers exactly where their employees are.
- GPS-equipped cars can tell rental-car companies if their cars are outside an agreed-on travel area.
- GPS-equipped cars can inform rental-car companies or employers if any of the vehicles in their fleet are exceeding the speed limit.
- GPS is now available for people who want to wear a wrist-sized device for quick navigation. Some GPS devices sell for less than one hundred fifty dollars.
- GPS provides directions in cars or cell phones to specific locations such as a restaurant, gas station, or hospital.

- Sportsmen widely use GPS to keep them from getting lost and to take them back to their favorite fishing or hunting spot.

- Finance companies use GPS to track the location of vehicles. The technology also allows finance companies to prevent the vehicle from starting if the payment is late.

- GPS is the technology used by OnStar, the security system developed by General Motors and built into some of its vehicles.

Just look at the growth of the number of vehicles using OnStar[5]:

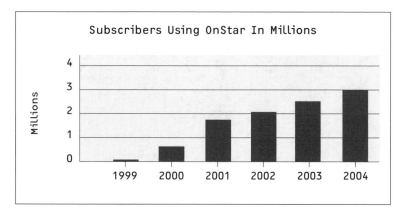

The most important question is not how many OnStar systems are in use, but how is GPS related to financial transactions?

On the surface most would not see a relationship; however, it is very related, as I'll explain in a moment.

Multipurpose Device

I believe that we are headed toward the use of a central or common device that will be able to:

- Identify you
- Verify *who* you say you are
- Authorize financial transactions
- Confirm you are *where* you say you are

Financial fraud could be eliminated 100 percent if a system could accomplish all the above. That's because the system could easily verify the location of the store and that you are actually the person in that store making the purchase. A foolproof system!

Note the connection to GPS: The system would be able to verify that *you* are actually at the specific location where the financial transaction is being made.

Adding GPS to our discussion is very appropriate as we approach a cashless society. Whether the GPS device is in a cell phone, watch, or an implantable computer chip—the problem with an invasion of privacy comes if consumers do not have the ability to turn GPS tracking devices off or on.

GPS is only going to grow in use and popularity. Be looking for a very public battle between proponents and opponents. GPS has great potential to be used for good, but invasion-of-privacy groups are sounding alarms that it can be used for harm.

This leads us to our next controversial topic: **What are biometrics, and should I be concerned with their use?**

CONTROVERSIAL ISSUE #5: BIOMETRICS

"Today, you pay with the click of a mouse—tomorrow, with the blink of an eye."[6]

"Biometrics are automated methods of recognizing a person based on a physiological or behavioral characteristic. Among the features measured are face, fingerprints, hand geometry, handwriting, iris, retina, vein, and voice. Biometric technologies are becoming the foundation of an extensive array of highly secure identification and personal verification solutions. As the level of security breaches and transaction fraud increases, the need for highly secure identification and personal verification technologies becomes apparent. Biometric-based solutions are able to provide for confidential financial transactions and personal data privacy."[7]

It appears that the use of biometrics will play a significant role in the healthy growth of a global economy. Whether we like it or not, biometrics is about to invade every aspect of our home, work, travel, and financial life.

WHY BIOMETRICS?

There are several convincing reasons we should note:

1. The use of biometrics for personal authentication is far more accurate than current authentication, like typing in a password or providing your Social Security number.

2. Biometric authentication is based on verifiable characteristics that only one individual possesses. For example, you can type in someone else's password, but you cannot duplicate the person's iris.

3. It's convenient. Nothing to remember, nothing to carry around, nothing to lose, nothing anyone else can steal.

Biometrics can be used in two ways. The first is identification—"who is this person?" The second is verification—"Is this person who he claims to be?"

Biometrics is used today in a variety of ways:

- **Hand geometry.** The first biometric technology to become widely accepted and used was hand geometry. A hand would be scanned to record such characteristics as shape, size, and finger length.

- **Fingerprints.** Another common use of biometrics is fingerprints. The problem with fingerprints is that approximately 5 percent of people do not have readable fingerprints. So fingerprints are not a valid option for biometric verification or identification. However, in 2003, finger scans accounted for about 60 percent of identification biometric technology being used. Facial scans were second at 23 percent. On January 5, 2004, the U.S. Department of Homeland Security began scanning fingerprints of foreigners entering the United States.

- **Iris and retina scanning.** Iris scanning seems to be the most reliable biometric method of the two.

- **Voice recognition.** It's cheap but not very reliable.

- **Gait recognition.** It attempts to recognize people from the way they walk.

- **Signature recognition.** This analyzes the way the pen moves when a signature is written.

- **Thermal imaging.** It seeks to identify people by the pattern of heat their bodies emit.

- **Multibiometrics.** In the long run, we will probably have to use multibiometrics, or several methods at a time.

HOW DOES BIOMETRICS WORK?

For example, some supermarkets are using biometrics. The customers allow the store to scan their fingerprints, which will be retained in the store's computer database. In addition, the customer also provides either a credit card number or checking account number for payment.

When customers make purchases, they have their fingerprints scanned, authentication is verified, and funds are transferred into the merchant's account. The customers do not have to write a check, sign a credit card receipt, show their driver's licenses, or answer any questions.

Some biometric fingerprinting scanners sell for as low as $39.95 and will work with most point-of-sale terminals already on the market.

In some test sites, the major malfunction has been the inability of the scanner to identify a registered customer. Why? It is possible the customer's fingerprint has dry or cracked skin or has very shallow ridges.

"In a two-year test by a leading financial institution, biometrics was preferred as the new payment technology by 75 percent of the participants, compared to 18 percent who preferred a chip card, and 3 percent who preferred a PDA."[8]

Biometrics is not getting as much press as, say, the VeriChip. Biometrics uses only the natural attributes that God has given us at birth. Nothing has to be implanted, nor does biometrics send out radio signals loaded with personal information.

Consumers appear to be more comfortable with the use of biometrics simply because it is natural.

It is my opinion that biometrics will grow in use and eventually become the primary means of identification, verification, and authorization of financial transactions.

Now that we have looked at RFID technology, computers, implantable computer chips, personal tracking devices, global positioning satellites, and biometrics, the next logical question is, **"Are there any benefits to living in a cashless society?"**

Yes, there really are some benefits!

In fact, many convincing arguments can be presented for the benefits of a cashless society. In the following chapter we will look at the most popular arguments and my analysis of each argument.

[1] Jane Black, "Roll Up Your Sleeve—for a Chip Implant," *Business Week Online*, March 22, 2002.

[2] Beth Bacheldor, "RFID Kick-Start," *Information Week,* May 24, 2004. www.informationweek.com/story/showArticle.jhtml?articleID=20900361.

[3] CNET News.com, July 28, 2004. http://news.zdnet.co.uk/hardware/emeringtech/0,39020357,39161907,00.htm.

[4] Applied Digital press release, October 13, 2004, http://www.adsx.com.

[5] http://onstar.internetpressroom.com (December 16, 2004 press release).

[6] Carl Pascarella, Visa USA President and CEO (National Association of College and University Business Officials' Annual Meeting, New York, NY, July 30, 2001).

[7] http://www.biometrics.org/html/introduction.html.

[8] http://www.paybytouch.com/company.html.

The Benefits

Are there any benefits of living in a cashless society?

YOU MUST BE THINKING, *Surely there are some benefits for a cashless society.* Yes, my research uncovered some very convincing benefits. In a "perfect world," going cashless could make the world a better place to live. However, we don't live in a perfect world.

Let's begin by looking at one of the most convincing benefits.

Benefit #1: DECREASE IN CRIMES RELATED TO MONEY

"It was about seven-thirty on a beautiful summer Tuesday night. We had just finished eating at our favorite restaurant. As we were walking back to our car, we were laughing and having a great time. Then suddenly, a man appeared from behind an old blue van. At first we were startled, and even hesitated for a moment. Before we could take one step forward, the man pulled a gun from his pocket and began pointing it at us.

He handed me a paper bag and said, 'Give me what I want; no one will get hurt. Put all your wallets into the bag, and give it to me.' Then he yelled out, 'Right now! Do it!'"

"The time was 9:05 a.m. The bank lobby doors had just been opened. We were all at our teller stations when a woman wearing a baseball cap, large sunglasses, and a heavy coat walked in. She immediately walked to my window and handed me a note saying, 'Put all the money from your drawer into the bag. If you sound an alarm, you're dead!' I immediately pushed the silent alarm button to alert the security guards and police that a robbery was in progress. I filled the bag with money and handed it to her. Out of the corner of my eye I noticed two security guards approaching the woman. She panicked, pulled out her pistol and shot both of the guards, one in the chest and the other in the right arm. Alarms were going off, and I could hear police car sirens in the distance. She immediately ran outside."

The stories above are fictional but represent composite accounts of real incidents played out every day in cities around the world. What was the motivation for each of these crimes? Money.

As I told these two stories to my friends, they immediately asked:

How many crimes are linked directly to money? I responded, "Great question." After doing significant research, here is what I came up with.

The 2004 Uniform Crime Report is not yet available, but according to the FBI's 2003 Uniform Crime Reporting (UCR) for the United States, currency stolen during 2003 amounted to $947,441,557. That's almost one billion dollars!

A cashless society would lead to a ...

- Decrease in murders
- Decrease in robberies of banks, stores, and people in streets and parking lots
- Decrease in thefts from homes and coin-operated machines
- Total elimination of counterfeiting
- Total elimination of bad checks
- Elimination of money laundering due to drug trafficking

Without any cash at banks, stores, homes, or on people, what incentive would there be to rob a person, bank, or store?

What is the crook going to say and do? Is he going to walk into a bank and wave his or her smart card or right arm with an implanted chip and say, "Stick em up and transfer all your money into my account"?

I don't think so. We know for a fact that cash robberies would be completely eliminated, because there would be no cash!

However, my friend Mike made this interesting prediction. He said, "Ethan, I believe more money will be stolen in a cashless society than in a cash society. In a cashless society, you can get to all of it, without having to be there physically."

For every new security device invented, there will always be a computer hacker who will be able to crack the code. Today, we have physical safe crackers; in the future we will have e-bank code crackers.

How about murders related to money?

MURDER

According to the latest statistics in the UCR data, 14,408 murders were recorded during the year 2003, and 1,397 of them were reported as being related to money issues.

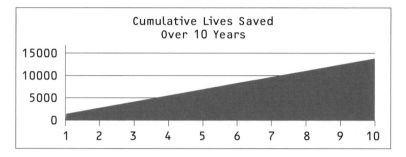

Cumulative Lives Saved Over 10 Years

A cashless society could have saved about fourteen hundred lives in 2003 and approximately fourteen thousand over a ten-year period.

Next, let's look specifically at the 2003 numbers for robbery.

ROBBERY: 413,402 robberies were committed.

Robbery accounted for:	29.9 percent of all violent crimes
Robbery offenders took:	estimated $514 million from their victims
Bank robberies:	average loss of $4,767 per robbery
Retail robberies:	average loss of $1,778 per robbery
Residential robberies:	average loss of $1,472 per robbery
Streets/highway robberies:	average loss of $898 per robbery
Convenience store robberies:	average loss of $813 per robbery
Gas station robberies:	average loss of $690 per robbery
Other robberies:	average loss of $1,258 per robbery
Pocket picking:	average loss of $294 per event
Purse snatching:	average loss of $367 per event
Coin operated machines:	average loss of $262 per event

43.4 percent of all robberies occurred on a street or highway

THE Benefits

Notice this last statistic: 43.4 percent of all robberies occur on the street or highway. What do you think they are after? Of course, cash!

If this analysis is true, a cashless society could have eliminated 179,416 robberies in 2003! (43.4 percent of 413,402 = 179,416.)

What about burglaries?

BURGLARIES

Losses due to burglaries totaled an estimated **$3.5 billion** in 2003.

Not all burglaries are of cash, but burglars surely are looking for cash and valuable property. A cashless society would certainly eliminate some of the burglaries, especially by those on drugs looking for money to purchase more drugs. But even a cashless society will not be able to eliminate the selling of stolen property. Unfortunately, crooks will still be able to complete cashless transactions, even for stolen goods.

KIDNAPPINGS

Many kidnappings are motivated by the potential to extort large sums of money from families, businesses, or governments. Without the ability to receive payments in cash, the kidnapper loses.

SUMMARY

In 2003, one murder took place every 31.8 minutes, one robbery every 1.3 seconds, and one burglary every 14.6 seconds.

The motivation for many crimes in America and globally is money, and a cashless society removes this motivation. Retailers, bankers, and consumers can all agree on this one! The only loser is the robber. In fact, he even wins because this will keep him from serving a few years behind bars!

The reduction and elimination of "physical" crime is a very convincing argument for a cashless society. In fact, it may be one of the most convincing arguments on the table.

As I spent time talking with my friends, at some point the topic of money management in a cashless society came up. They asked, "Will a cashless society make it easier or harder to manage our money?"

Benefit #2: Improved Money Management

Most believe that a cashless society will create improved cash management. How many times have you cashed a check for fifty dollars, only to realize in a few days your wallet is empty, and you have no idea where you spent the money?

In a cashless society, everything will be documented. That's right; you will be able to know exactly how much you spent eating out last month, how much you spent on ice cream or at a Starbucks coffee shop. With advancing technology, all your expenses will even be categorized for your budget: giving, housing, food, transportation, children, and insurance. The "itemization" in your reports will be as specific (name of store) or as general (food) as you want it to be.

Now here is the exciting part! When you are close to reaching your food or clothing budget limit, you might receive an e-mail or a message on your cell phone or watch stating, "Food budget is at 90 percent."

Just think how helpful this aspect could be for families in the area of money management.

From a cash management perspective, cashless is good—if you can control your spending—because you'll receive more detailed records and budgeting advantages. The retailers will not like this aspect because you might not be spending money you have not budgeted! The real advantage goes to the consumer on this one! I can see some positive advantages for a cashless society in improved money management. This is also a very convincing argument.

Benefit #3: No Lost Cash

I remember several years ago I misplaced a considerable amount of money. Well, for me it was considerable. I remember searching in my closet, my shirt pockets, my coat pockets, my car, the entire house, my briefcase, and my wallet.

Have you ever lost any money? I am sure most of us have at some time. Well, a cashless society would eliminate the potential to lose any cash, because there would be no cash to lose.

Benefit #4: Faster Transactions

All retail establishments want to help you pay for your purchases in the most efficient and fastest way possible.

Years ago, it took over one minute to process credit card transactions. That time was reduced to thirty seconds, and now it can be accomplished in seven seconds or less!

With the present technology, it takes less time to process cashless transactions than it does to make change for a twenty-dollar bill!

Speed of transaction is a major argument or selling point for retailers and consumers. The long-term aspect of a cashless society is that we will no longer be swiping cards and having to wait even seven seconds. In reality, if RFID technology continues to develop and become widespread, processing transactions will become practically instantaneous. All we will have to do is wave our card, watch, or arm, and the total of our purchases will be deducted from our bank account or charged to our credit card.

BENEFIT #5: INCREASED NATIONAL SECURITY

Another strong argument for a cashless society is increased national security. As the theory goes, if you can track the purchases and track the money to whoever controls the account, you can eliminate the terrorist.

A cashless society will help in the fight against terrorists. Cash can easily finance terrorist activities, because little or no means exists to trace from whom or where it came. However, in a cashless society, cash is eliminated, and everything is traceable.

It's a fact. Cash is hard to trace, and electronic transactions are traceable—especially if nations begin using biometrics for verifying and identifying individuals regarding existing accounts or in opening new accounts.

BENEFIT #6: CONVENIENCE

Just think about how convenient living in a cashless society would be.

- No cash to worry about losing or being stolen
- Ease of transactions—simple and fast

- No checkbooks to haul around
- No having to order expensive checks
- No checks to write!

Many people believe that cashless is simpler. I would tend to agree with them. With everything being electronic, life has the potential to be less confusing—especially in the financial area.

No more trips to the bank to deposit your paycheck. No more trips to the bank or ATM to withdraw cash. No more having to track your income and expenses, because it will all be computerized.

As the transition continues, expect major marketing campaigns to pour millions of dollars into convincing you how great cashless can be. And I believe consumers can and eventually will be convinced that cashless is better.

In the first five chapters of *Cashing It In,* I have tried to answer the following questions:

- Why do you need to be on the alert and ready concerning a cashless society?
- How far along are we to becoming a cashless society?
- What is the technology driving a cashless society?
- What are the privacy concerns in a cashless society?
- What are the benefits of living in a cashless society?

Now, for the last part of *Cashing It In,* I am going to look toward the future and answer the following questions:
- How can I best prepare for a cashless society? What should I be doing?
- As I prepare, what things should I not be doing?

- What will the future look like in a cashless society?
- What does the Bible have to say about a cashless society?
- What are my responsibilities as a Christian?

Let's begin with what you can be doing to prepare for a cashless society.

CHAPTER 6

The Preparation

what should I be doing?

AS I HAVE DISCUSSED *Cashing It In* with my friends, family, and associates, most of them wanted to know what they should be doing to prepare. They wanted answers to questions like:

> **"How can I best prepare to live in a cashless society?"**
>
> **"How can I avoid identity theft?"**
>
> **"How can I learn to manage my money without checks and cash?"**

They wanted me to give them a specific list of things to be doing. Based on my research, what was I doing, and what directives could I provide for them?

In other words, "Give me a checklist!"

In response to these questions I have come up with a list of dos and don'ts. I will be presenting the dos in this chapter and the don'ts in the following chapter.

My list will not only help you today in a cash society but will be equally helpful in a cashless society! The primary concerns are protecting yourself from identity theft and fraudulent charges on your account.

ethan's list of dos

1. Do purchase a commercial paper shredder for your home and office and shred any financial and important papers you're discarding.

A paper shredder in your home has more value to you than your refrigerator or washing machine. Don't waste your money buying an inexpensive home shredder for $29.95. I burned out one of those cheap ones and had to buy another one. Go out and buy a good one. View it as an investment in your privacy and financial security. Most good commercial units will cost over one hundred dollars and will be able to easily shred at least ten sheets of paper at one time. What you don't want to do is have to stand there and feed in one sheet at a time. I tried it and quit using it. I also recommend that you purchase a shredder that cross cuts into confetti. Do not purchase one that simply shreds your documents into long strips of paper.

You do not want your name, Social Security number, and address in the wrong hands. Never trash any credit card application unless you shred it first.

By shredding every piece of mail before it hits the trash can, you will be able to avoid what is known as "dumpster diving." Dumpster diving takes place in commercial locations and in the trash cans outside your house.

2. Do have your driver's license ID changed.

Many states use your Social Security number for your driver's license number. However, if you ask, most states will allow you to stop using your Social Security number and obtain a unique driver's license number. The next time you have to renew your license, be sure to have your number changed. By the way, there should not be any additional cost for you to do this. Remind other members of your family to do the same.

Why change your number? Typically, whenever you write a check the vendor writes your driver's license number, Social Security number, and birth date on your check. Numerous people will view your check and your Social Security number—the sales clerk, the person making the deposit, the bank teller and bank proofers, and so on.

Finding and using a person's Social Security number is the #1 ingredient required to create a false identity.

3. Do reconcile and review your bank statement every month.

During the last few months I have been helping my mother reconcile her bank statement each month. One month I noticed an electronic transfer of about two hundred dollars on her bank statement. I later discovered that it had not been an approved expense. Thankfully, we were able to recover all the money.

If I had not been reviewing and reconciling her bank statement each month, this transfer would have gone unnoticed. If the crook saw that he or she got away with it once, you can be assured more unauthorized transfers would take place in the future. Unless you reconcile your bank statement each month, how do you know this has not been happening to you, your parents, someone in your family, or someone you know? The fact is you don't!

4. *Do review your credit card statement every month.*

Just as important as reconciling your bank statement each month, you need to carefully review each credit card statement.

How do you do this? Whenever I make a credit card purchase I always put the receipt in one place: my wallet. My wife keeps all her receipts in her purse. At the end of each week, I place all my credit card receipts in my credit card folder. When the bill arrives, I look at each item on the statement and place a check next to the dollar amount if I have a receipt documenting the charge. If I do not have a receipt, I do more investigating. It is possible I lost a receipt, but very unlikely. Next, I check my calendar to see if this would help me remember making a charge at a specific restaurant or gas station. If I cannot find any documentation of my charge, I then call the credit card company and ask them to research the charge and provide me the proper documentation.

Without reviewing your credit card statement, how do you know the clerk at the gas station you regularly use is not running a twenty-dollar charge on your account each month? Unless you review and verify your statement, you don't know if this is happening!

If your credit card bill or bank statements do not arrive as scheduled, call the institution immediately. It is possible someone requested a change of address for your account. You might be asking, "So what?" It's a big so what, because the crook has bought several weeks of time to make more purchases before you know unauthorized charges or debits are being made.

5. *Do keep a list of all your credit card and debit card numbers.*

If you lose your wallet or it is stolen, you need to contact your financial institution and report the missing cards. You will need your numbers. On this same piece of paper, it would be helpful to have the phone number you need to call. Of course, you will need to keep this paper in a secure location.

At the writing of this book, the cardholder's responsibility for unauthorized credit card charges is limited to fifty dollars. The limits are different for ATM or debit cards. Be sure to check with your card company for the exact details for your card.

However, the following are generally true:

- If you report the card as lost before anyone uses it, you cannot be held responsible.
- If you report the lost card within two business days, you could be responsible for up to fifty dollars.
- If you report the lost card within sixty days, you could be responsible for up to five hundred dollars.
- If you fail to report a lost card, you risk unlimited loss.

6. Do pay your credit card bill in full every month.

One of the problems with a cashless society is that people spend more if they don't use cash to make purchases. Some retail establishments have documented that consumers spend an average of 33 percent more when using plastic.

Did you realize that if you charged five hundred dollars and made only the minimum payment, depending on your interest rate, it could take you anywhere from twelve to twenty years to pay off your balance? That is nonsense and definitely not good stewardship.

Do you pay your credit card bill in full each month? If not, how many years have you been keeping a balance? One year? Five years? Ten years? Twenty-five years?

7. Do purchase and use a "wipe clean" program.

Did you know that even after you delete a file, a technically skilled person could find it on your computer? Only a wipe clean software program will ensure that the file you deleted is really deleted! I realize this sounds strange, but it's true! Your deleted file can be recovered in some cases. This is the reason the FBI confiscates computers during most investigations. Why? They are looking to find files or "deleted files" with critical information on the computer.

8. Do check your credit report annually.

I strongly recommend that you check your credit report on an annual basis. Go ahead and get into a routine of checking it at the beginning of every New Year or maybe on your birthday. Federal law provides that all three credit-reporting companies provide a report annually at no charge. This provision is becoming available on a rollout schedule by region of the country. Check the Web site www.annualcreditreport.com to learn when free reports will be available in your part of the United States. Experts recommend staggering your requests from the three companies throughout the year, rather than checking all three at once, so you can keep tabs on your credit accounts several times during the year. Links to all three companies are available on the Web site.

What are you looking for?

- To see if you have any active credit cards or debit cards that you are not using or do not know about. If you do, close them immediately.

- To see if you have any untrue comments on your report. If you find one, and you can verify that it is indeed not true, contact the credit bureau by sending a letter by certified mail.

- To see if someone has taken a loan out in your name without your knowing it. It is possible that someone stole your identity, obtained a loan, provided a bogus address, and your loan is now in default—and you never even knew it.

In my opinion, the least important reason to be checking your credit report is to find out your credit score. If you always pay your bills on time, you will have a great score. If you are always late, your score will be low, and no one should be loaning you any additional money! Loan denials protect not only the lender but also *you*.

The three credit rating companies are:

Equifax	www.equifax.com
Experian	www.experian.com
TransUnion	www.transunion.com

You can also check my Web site for additional information on this topic: www.foundationsforliving.org.

9. Do find the best credit card for you.

There is not one card that is a perfect fix for every family. You have to determine what you are looking for...

- Frequent flyer miles?
- Low interest rates?
- Cash rebates?
- No annual fees?

If you are trying to get out of credit card debt, you need to find companies offering low interest rates. If you are debt free, you are looking for "benefits" and a card with no annual fee. Be sure to check out our Web site for helpful articles in this area.

10. Do find a bank that offers online banking and begin using the service.

Go ahead and find a bank that offers free online banking and bill paying. What are you waiting for? Take the plunge and begin learning the system. It does not mean you have to begin paying all your bills online, but at least begin paying one or two each month, just to see how it works. Once you see how simple it is and that it actually works, you will be eager to pay all your bills online and wonder why it took you so long to discover this opportunity.

Be sure you take advantage of all the benefits of Internet banking!

- Bill paying
- Ability to check your account balance
- Automatic or manual transfers between accounts
- Direct mortgage payments
- Direct deposit for your paychecks
- Order new checks (until we all stop using checks)

11. Do become 100 percent debt free.

I have been saying for over twenty years that one of the best things a family can do is to work toward becoming 100 percent free of debt—including your home mortgage. Cashless society or not, this is a good plan.

In a cash or cashless society, being debt free brings great freedom. No matter what happens in the economy, you will own your home and have a place to live. For those who are on this earth during the last days when everyone is required to receive the mark of the Beast (Rev. 13:16) to buy, sell, and make mortgage payments— you could be in trouble if you do not own your home. As a believer, you will not choose to worship the Beast and receive the mark of the Beast. (See chapter 9 for a fuller discussion.) Therefore, you will not be able to make your mortgage payment, and the bank will foreclose on your home.

12. Do prepare your family and friends.

In an intelligent, logical, and biblical manner, be sure that every member of your family and your friends at church are informed concerning the coming cashless society. Provide them with important facts, or give them a copy of this book.

Ask your pastor if he will give a series of sermons on the coming cashless society. This series could be a great evangelistic tool to reach your neighbors for Christ.

13. Do stay informed.

Monitor any developing issues that appear associated with a cashless society. I recommend that you monitor the issues I have listed below. In time, some could be dropped off the list, and others will need to be added. Visit www.foundationsforliving.org for an updated list.

A. RFID
This is the developing technology that most likely will play a major role in a cashless society. Currently, the range for scanning an RFID tag can be just inches to fifty feet, if the tag is active. Be on the alert for developing technology that will allow a passive RFID tag to be read from more than fifty feet away. This could lead to an invasion of privacy as we have never seen before. Just by carrying a smart card in your wallet, your every move could be monitored.

B. VERICHIP
Keep up with developing stories about implanting computer chips into the body. Are there health concerns? Is the chip removable? What are the potential benefits? Can the chip be deactivated and reactivated at any time? What type of data will be stored on the chip that potentially can be read or scanned without your knowledge?

C. GPS
It appears that the Global Positioning System could play a role in a complex system that will be used to verify your location and approve financial transactions. Keep your eye on what is being said about the use of GPS. The system could be used for good or evil.

D. BIOMETRICS
Biometrics is the use of personal characteristics such as fingerprints and your iris to identify you. We have only

scratched the surface in the future use of biometrics for financial transactions and national security. Be watching for a combined use of smart chip technology and biometrics in the future. I believe the expanded use of biometrics is a good thing.

E. INTERNET BANKING

We all need to be aware of what is going on in Internet banking, or e-banking. Banking using your desktop computer, laptop, PDA, or cell phone will become more common each year.

14. Do know the terms and level of risk involved in using the Internet.

For example, do you know what spam is? How about a Trojan horse or spyware? Let's look at the definitions I found at www.webopedia.com for a few important terms you need to know.

Spam: Electronic junk mail or junk newsgroup postings. Some people define spam even more generally as any unsolicited e-mail. However, if a long-lost brother finds your e-mail address and sends you a message, this could hardly be called spam, even though it's unsolicited. Real spam is generally e-mail advertising for some product sent to a mailing list or newsgroup.

Trojan horse: One of the most insidious types of Trojan horse is a program that claims to rid your computer of viruses but instead introduces viruses onto your computer.

Spyware: Any software that covertly gathers user information through the user's Internet connection without his or her knowledge, usually for advertising purposes.

Spyware applications are typically bundled as a hidden component of freeware or shareware programs that can be downloaded from the Internet; note, however, that the majority of shareware and freeware applications do not come with spyware. Once installed, the spyware monitors user activity on the Internet and transmits that information in the background to someone else. Spyware can also gather information about e-mail addresses and even passwords and credit card numbers.

Virus: A program or piece of code that is loaded onto your computer without your knowledge and runs against your wishes. Viruses can also replicate themselves. All computer viruses are man-made. A simple virus that can make a copy of itself over and over again is relatively easy to produce. Even such a simple virus is dangerous because it will quickly use all available memory and bring the system to a halt. An even more dangerous type of virus is one capable of transmitting itself across networks and bypassing security systems.

You must be proactive in this area of your life! Plan into your schedule to take an hour and learn about the Internet, your computer, and the Web. Once again, a great place to learn is www.webopedia.com.

Your goal is to stay informed and keep on the alert!

important things to do checklist

- ❏ Purchase a commercial paper shredder.
- ❏ Have your driver's license ID changed (if using SS number).
- ❏ Reconcile and review your bank statement every month.
- ❏ Review your credit card statement every month.
- ❏ Keep a list of all your credit card and debit card numbers.
- ❏ Pay your credit card bill in full every month.
- ❏ Purchase and use a "wipe clean" software program.
- ❏ Check your credit report annually.
- ❏ Find the best credit card.
- ❏ Find a bank that offers online banking, and begin using it.
- ❏ Become 100 percent debt free.
- ❏ Prepare your family and friends.
- ❏ Stay informed.
- ❏ Know the terms and level of risk in using the Internet.

CHAPTER 7

The cautions

what should I not be doing?

THERE ARE A NUMBER OF SEEMINGLY ordinary activities that we should not be doing because of the security risks they pose! I have tried to be as specific and direct as possible. I consider everything on my list to be of the utmost importance today (in a cash society) and in the future (in a cashless society).

Following my advice cannot harm you, but you can **potentially be hurt** if you don't. Here goes...

Ethan's list of Don'ts

1. Don't just trash your old credit card, bank, or investment statements. For obvious reasons you should not simply throw away any statements with your name, address, and account number printed on them. Be sure you shred them first! The same is true for any piece of paper with personal data printed on it, like a credit card receipt.

2. Don't trash your mail without shredding it first.

To accomplish this you have to own a good shredder, as I mentioned in the previous chapter. (See dos list #1.) Be sure you buy one that can shred ten sheets of paper or unopened thick envelopes. You don't want shredding to be a time-consuming or frustrating event. The better the machine, the more likely you will use it!

3. Don't ever give personal financial data to anyone calling you.

Note the key point: to anyone *calling you.* The phone call might go something like this:

Caller: "Hi, is this Mr. Jones?"

Mr. Jones: "Yes."

Caller: "Mr. Jones, this is Sam Hoover calling from your bank. We are in the process of verifying the information in our computer system and need your assistance. Do you have a minute?"

Mr. Jones: "OK."

Caller: "Can you help us by providing your correct mailing address, phone number, and Social Security number?"

Here is what Mr. Jones should say:

Mr. Jones: "I tell you what I will do. The next time I am in the bank, I will be sure to update my information."

Caller: "But, Mr. Jones, if you don't verify your information today, we will have to make your account inactive. Now, I am sure you don't want that to happen."

Mr. Jones: CLICK!

What is the key factor in this situation?

They called you! Banks or credit card companies will **never** call you and ask for confidential information.

Let me repeat what I just said. Banks or credit card companies will **never** call you and ask for confidential information.

4. Don't ever give personal financial data in response to any e-mail you receive.

Lately I have been receiving e-mail from "recognizable financial institutions" asking me to click on the link and verify some important information. Often the e-mail will read, "If you do not respond to our request, your account will be closed in ten days."

Internet scammers are doing what has become known as "phishing." Phishing is when a crook creates a replica of an existing Web site to trick a user into submitting personal, financial, or password data.

NEVER click on a computer link and provide personal data. The only time you might give personal financial data is when you visit a Web site and you are making a purchase.

The e-mail might look official. The e-mail might have the real logo. The e-mail might sound legitimate—but it is not.

No legitimate financial institution is going to send you e-mail and ask you to respond by sending financial data or to click on a link and provide that data.

Note the key point in the last two points. *You* need to be the initiator.

5. Don't e-mail personal financial data in a regular e-mail.

Regular e-mail messages are not secure and can be viewed by many sets of eyes! For example, let's say your daughter (in college) needs to buy a new laptop computer.

Don't e-mail her your credit card information! Call on a phone and give her the information.

6. Don't use a computer without a secure firewall installed.

A firewall is simply software that helps keep your computer secure from intrusion. It attempts to do exactly what it says: Build a security wall around your data, so you won't get burned by an outsider raiding your computer and taking important data or injecting a destructive virus into your computer.

Every time you visit a Web site, it has the potential to deposit what is known as a cookie into your computer. This cookie will later send them information about *you*— like what Web sites you have visited, which tells them what interests you.

Have you ever visited a Web site that sells books? Ever done a search for a book by subject? Ever bought a book on a Web site? Well, I have. Every time I return to that site an ad might pop up that says, "You might be interested in these books." Why are most of them Christian books? Because that is what I have expressed interest in. Do you think they have a pop-up of Christian books for everyone? No way!

Hunters have sports books pop up!

NASCAR fans have racing books pop up!

That doesn't happen just by accident!

That cookie makes it happen.

You might be thinking, "Now wait a minute! I thought a cookie was something that I ate, not something in my computer." Let me give you the definition for *cookie* that I found on www.webopedia.com. Again, this is a great Web site to help you understand computer terms and how the Internet works.

"The main purpose of cookies is to identify users and possibly prepare customized Web pages for them. When you enter a Web site using cookies, you may be asked to fill out a form providing such information as your name and interests. This information is packaged into a cookie and sent to your Web browser, which stores it for later use. The next time you go to the same Web site, your browser will send the cookie to the Web server. The server can use this information to present you with custom Web pages. So, for example, instead of seeing just a generic welcome page you might see a welcome page with your name on it."

I might also add that a Web site could deposit cookies into your computer without your filling out a form!

A firewall becomes even more critical if your computer is always connected to the Internet. Without a firewall, a hacker could invade your computer, access private data, and even destroy all the files on your computer once he gets what he is looking for.

If you use a dial-up Internet connection to check your e-mail and browse a few Web sites for about fifteen minutes each day, your level of risk is lower. However, if you are connected to the Internet twenty-four hours a day, seven days a week (24/7), the potential for a hacker to break into your computer and steal personal data greatly increases!

7. Don't use a computer without antivirus software.

In the world of computer viruses, every computer needs to be protected with antivirus software. The cost is relatively inexpensive, and the daily updates are very simple to do. You can even schedule your computer to automatically update daily. Since new viruses are discovered practically every day, why not take full advantage of the service you are paying for and upgrade daily? It costs the same if you update daily or monthly!

8. Don't download files unless you know exactly whom they are from.

Never download a file from a stranger or unsolicited e-mail. If you open this file, you could obtain a virus, or the file could hijack your computer and modem for fraudulent activities.

9. Don't make purchases on the Internet without using a secure Web site.

A secure Web site will have a small yellow padlock symbol at the bottom of your computer screen. It's a little "lock" icon. This symbol indicates that the site is secure.

Also look and see if the URL for the Web site begins with "https:" The "s" stands for secure.

If it has a "lock" icon or "https," is the site 100 percent secure? Well, not 100 percent secure, but at least 99.9 percent. Crooks have even found ways to forge security icons.

10. Don't use common passwords for financial data.

Avoid using your Social Security number, birth date, or your middle name for passwords. Use what is known as a "strong" password that has letters and numbers that are in no way related to *you*. For example, create a password such as 184Sea97. Even try to use upper- and lowercase in your password.

11. Don't use automatic log-in features.

All you are doing is storing your log-in and password on your or their computer system. Your log-in and password should be stored in only one place—your brain!

12. Don't pay for Internet banking services.

I have noticed that some banks are offering Internet banking for free. If your bank is charging you a fee, you might consider banking somewhere else.

13. Don't carry numerous credit and debit cards in your wallet.

Keep your life simple. Use one credit card or at the most two! If you lose your wallet, you make two phone calls.

14. Don't automatically give out your Social Security number.

Ask if you can use your driver's license number or another number. Ask them why they need it. How will it be used? What will happen if you don't provide it?

15. Don't fear change.

Be willing to adjust. As I have mentioned before, there is nothing evil, wrong, or unbiblical about a cashless society. The problem arises when evil people control the "cashless system." We know this will be the case one day (Revelation 13).

16. Don't overspend.

One of the negative aspects of a totally cashless society will be overspending. This is already a problem in our current system, but it will become more of a problem in a cashless society. Why would I say this? Research has indicated that when people make noncash purchases, they usually spend more. Some fast-food restaurants are reporting that customers are spending 33 percent more when they do not use cash.

Even in a cashless society, banks will continue to offer overdraft protection. I am sure that, for some people, knowing this "safety net" is available could lead to overspending.

17. Don't ever click on the "unsubscribe" link in an e-mail message you receive, unless you know for certain that the company is legitimate.

Have you ever received e-mail from a person or company that you had no relationship with? We all have. Ever noticed at the bottom it says, "Click here to unsubscribe"? Baloney! It might as well read, "All fools click here." Don't do it unless you know it is a legitimate company.

Why? Here is what e-mail spammers do. They do not know your valid address; therefore, they send out seven e-mails with the following addresses:

johnsmith@emailnet.com

john@emailnet.com

jsmith@emailnet.com

js@emailnet.com

josmith@emailnet.com

johns@emailnet.com

jn@emailnet.com

Your correct address is js@emailnet.com. All the rest of the e-mails bounce back, and the good address arrives in your e-mail box.

You see "unsubscribe" and click on it. They receive your response, and now they know that this address is valid and sell your address to other spam companies!

18. Don't ever have your Social Security number printed on your checks or other documents.

Common sense tells you never to do this one. Social Security numbers are what most crooks use for identity theft. Don't make it easier for them by printing it on your check!

19. Don't put your credit card number on your payment check.

I know, I know, I know. The credit card company asks you to put your credit card number on the memo line when you are making a payment. In my opinion, too many eyes view my check. For over twenty-five years I have never written my credit card number on the memo line. I recommend that you don't do it either.

20. Don't mail letters from an unsecured location.

It is best not to leave your mail outside your home or even drop your mail in an unsecured drop box in the office. A crook might see a payment envelope to Visa and simply slip it into his pocket. He will probably mail the payment and request your address be changed to a bogus address to create several weeks of time before you notice *his* unauthorized charges to your credit card. If you don't receive your credit card bill in the mail (because it has been redirected to a bogus new address), you don't know someone has been making charges using your credit card number until weeks later.

21. Don't assume your family and friends won't steal your identity.

In 2004 there were 9.3 million new victims of identity fraud. This represents 4.3 percent of the U.S. adult population. Family, friends, and neighbors account for 50 percent of all known identity thieves.[1] Can you believe that? 50 percent!

21. Don't fall victim to free vacations!

If it sounds too good to be true, it probably is! Have you ever received a call and the person says, "You have been selected to receive a free ten-day vacation"? Well, first of all, once you spend some time talking, you'll usually be asked for a processing or travel membership fee. Some of these callers are only trying to obtain your credit card number, Social Security number, or bank account number.

They might say, "Sir, all I need for you to do in order for me to reserve your vacation package is cover the $9.95 handling fee. Would you like to put this on your credit card? Sir, what is that number?"

See how it works? The caller is not looking to trick you out of $9.95, but to trick you into giving him your credit card or Social Security number. They have aspirations that far exceed $9.95.

REMEMBER: NEVER GIVE OUT FINANCIAL DATA UNLESS YOU MAKE THE PHONE CALL!

22. Don't become a victim of scams.

How many times have you received the "Nigerian" e-mail letter asking for your help? Once again, if they are offering free money, there is only one thing you need to do: Hit the delete button.

I recently read an article on the Federal Trade Commission Web site (www.ftc.gov) documenting that the Nigerian e-mail scam letter has reached "epidemic" proportions. According to the article, some who have responded in hope of a big financial payout have actually been beaten, threatened, and in some cases murdered.

And literally the most important advice I can give you concerning the coming cashless society…

23. Don't ever agree to have a mark placed on your forehead or right hand.

See chapter 9 for more information.

Finally, let me invite you to visit my Web site for updated checklists, a "cashless readiness" test, and other new and helpful information. Go to www.foundationsforliving.org.

[1] *Hattiesburg American,* January 29, 2005, D3.

IMPORTANT THINGS CHECKLIST

- ❑ Don't trash your old credit card, bank, or investment statements.
- ❑ Don't trash your mail without shredding it first.
- ❑ Don't ever give out personal financial data to anyone calling you.
- ❑ Don't ever give personal financial data in response to any e-mail you receive.
- ❑ Don't e-mail personal financial data in a regular e-mail.
- ❑ Don't use a computer without a secure firewall installed.
- ❑ Don't use a computer without antivirus software.
- ❑ Don't download files unless you know exactly whom they are from.
- ❑ Don't make purchase on the Internet without using a secure Web site.
- ❑ Don't use common passwords for financial data.
- ❑ Don't use automatic log-in features.
- ❑ Don't pay for Internet banking services.
- ❑ Don't carry numerous credit and debit cards in your wallet.

- ❑ Don't automatically give out your Social Security number.

- ❑ Don't fear change.

- ❑ Don't overspend.

- ❑ Don't ever click on the "unsubscribe" link on an e-mail message you receive, unless you know for certain that the company is legitimate.

- ❑ Don't ever have your Social Security number printed on your checks or other documents.

- ❑ Don't write your credit card number on the memo line.

- ❑ Don't mail letters from an unsecured location.

- ❑ Don't assume your family and friends won't steal your identity.

- ❑ Don't fall victim to free vacations (obtain credit card number trick).

- ❑ Don't become a victim of scams (example "Nigerian e-mail mail").

- ❑ Don't ever agree to have a mark placed on your forehead or right hand.

The forecast

what will the transition to and future in a cashless society look like?

HOW CLOSE ARE WE TO BECOMING A CASHLESS SOCIETY? I am not a prophet, so it would be foolish on my part to project a date when our country and the world will become cashless. With that said, I am willing to go on record saying that, as I have analyzed the data, the evidence is indisputable that one day we will have a cashless society.

During the last two years we have seen an explosion in people's interest in and use of debit cards and contact-less payment devices. I expect this exponential growth to continue as months and years pass.

How soon before all cash disappears?

There will have to be a transition period before cash is totally eliminated. Two key requisites will be consumer confidence and a government mandate.

Once consumer acceptance is widespread and cashless transactions are basically the norm, I expect our government will pass legislation to remove all currency from our economy.

what can we expect to happen in the next few years as the transition begins?

Let me summarize my response with the following observations:

- We will see technological developments as we have never seen before, with new gadgets and faster technology that would even amaze Dick Tracy.

- We will see controversial developments that will provoke moral and spiritual debates over their proposed use. Example: Implantable computer chips.

- In future elections, the debate over a cashless society will become a major issue. Senior citizens will oppose it, while the younger generation will embrace it.

- We will see a massive public marketing campaign to convince consumers to stop using cash and checks and enjoy the benefits of going cashless.

- The transition will be fast moving, with more things happening than the year before, but taking years to fully implement.

- New laws concerning the Internet will be passed and enforced by our government—laws that we do not have today, I might add. I have a friend who operates an Internet service. He told me that someone breached his security and took over one of his computers! When he called the FBI they said, "Unless you prove that the hacker caused you $100,000 in damage, we are not going to do anything about it." I believe that now the minimum damage requirement has been lowered to $10,000. It's hard to believe that you can be charged for stealing a $10 item at Wal-Mart, but it takes over $10,000 in computer damage before the FBI will get involved.

- As the transition continues, we will see a decrease in "physical" crimes related to money, and this trend will be used to convince consumers to accept a totally cashless society. However, we will begin to see an increase in cyber crimes! Cashless will not eliminate financial crimes!

- A cashless economy will also become the focus of major terrorist attacks—to hack the system or to try to destroy the system.

- The craving for world peace due to increasing terrorist attacks will induce consumers to compromise privacy.

- It is apparent that consumers will experience a growing invasion of privacy and greater abuse of privacy.

- At some point, we will have a final deadline—that our nation is going cashless.

- At some point, the global community will establish a final deadline—that the world is going cashless. We will see some type of an international proclamation or mandate with every nation signing on and agreeing to join the cashless society. I can only assume the United Nations might play a role in drafting this document.

what things must happen before we have a cashless society?

In my opinion, four key trends must all be moving forward.

First, we must have the *technological ability* for it to happen. We already have the computer power and the global financial network in place. You can almost check this one off your list. √

Second, the *retailers must be in favor of the change.* We are already seeing unprecedented movement in this area with major retailers like McDonald's. You can almost check this one off your list. √

Third, without a *high level of consumer acceptance,* a cashless society would never happen. Consumers appear to be climbing on board in great numbers. Consumers are now using plastic more than writing checks. You can almost check this one off your list. √

Finally, the *government must give some form of approval* for a cashless society to become a reality. I have already documented that the government is fully behind the trend to go cashless and will in my opinion become the first institution to go 100 percent cashless. You can almost check this one off your list. √

We are close, but not there yet!

what will the future look like in a cashless society?

While I am not a prophet, nor am I attempting to be a prophet, I would like to offer several predictions concerning what life might look like in a cashless society—all based on hundreds of hours of diligent research and good old common sense.

You might be asking what qualifies Ethan Pope to be so bold as to make such predictions. First, it would be important for you to understand that I have devoted the last twenty years of my life to researching, studying, writing, and teaching in the area of finance. In addition, I have a business degree in accounting, a business background, a master's degree from Dallas Theological Seminary, and I am a CERTIFIED FINANCIAL PLANNER.

I realize that making predictions can be a dangerous thing to do, but in the case of this book, I believe it is an important thing to do—to give you a realistic glimpse into the future.

For some of the following predictions you might say, "Well, duh, of course that is going to happen," while for others you might be somewhat surprised at my conclusions.

In a cashless society we will have:

1. No cash or coins. All transactions will be electronic.

2. No paper checking accounts. This is almost the case now among college students. Debit cards are the preferred method of payment.

3. Global economy. You will be able to buy or sell anything to anyone, anywhere in the world.

4. Global hot spot. You will be able to connect to the Internet anywhere in the world at any time.

5. Paperless economy. The cashless society will be virtually paperless.

6. Internet predominance. Internet use will grow and become a primary tool in the buying and selling of goods. The Internet structure will also be a target for terrorist attacks.

7. Biotech. Thanks to the use of biotech (iris scans or hand scans), we will no longer have to remember and use log-in names and passwords.

8. Implantable computer chips. Some type of implantable computer chip will be used to store health and financial data. It will be widely accepted around the world.

9. ATM machines. Be watching for a peak, then a drop-off, in the use of ATMs, because this will signal that a cashless society is on the way. Why? Who needs an ATM machine when you don't need to use cash?

10. U.S. government all cashless. The U.S. government will be the first institution to become 100 percent cashless.

11. Buying groceries. When you finish your shopping, all you will have to do is push the entire cart through the checkout line. Because of RFID technology (as discussed in chapter 3), no scanning will be necessary. Instantly, your purchase total will be confirmed, and the funds will be electronically withdrawn from your bank account or charged to your credit card—based on your preference.

12. Online ordering. All you will have to do is fill up your electronic shopping card, hit the purchase button, and either insert your smart card or let your computer scan your fingerprint or iris, and the entire transaction is done!

13. Ultimate money management. In a cashless society we will have personal computer money managers that will automatically decide which bills to pay without our even having to make a decision. This smart money management technology will have the capability to prioritize, pay bills, and give you daily or weekly reports.

14. Loan approvals. In the future, computers will make loan approvals or denials without humans even being directly involved in the process. The instant transfer between computers of balance sheets, income statements, budgets, and spending habits will accelerate home mortgage and auto loan approvals. No more filling out long loan application forms! You will have the potential for hundreds of lending institutions to process your application and give you approval or denial. For all the loans approved, you will be able to see the top three loan offers available.

15. Gas purchases. In a cashless society, every gas station will allow you to drive up to a gas pump, wave your key chain, watch, or arm, and pump your gas. This aspect is already very popular today but is not offered at every gas station.

16. Kids' allowances. Your kids won't be asking for cash, but for you to transfer fifty dollars onto their e-cash card or transfer fifty dollars into their global e-cash account.

17. No plastic credit cards. Why? Thanks to biotech being used for identification verification, we will no longer need to keep plastic in our purse or wallet.

18. Digital invoices and bills. In a cashless society, paper invoices and bills will become extinct. All invoices and bills will be sent and paid electronically. No more stacks of paper!

19. Shopping lists. Your milk carton will automatically add itself to an electronic shipping list when the

RFID tag on the milk indicates the "expiration date" of the milk is reached. And, on your approval, your electronic shopping list will be transmitted to the online grocer who, in turn, will show up at your home with your order. All this will be done without your leaving your home or even making a phone call.

20. Payment notification. For safety purposes, you will have an electronic notice appear on your watch or cell phone every time a debit or credit hits your bank account. Let's say you go to a restaurant and pay with debit. Within seconds you receive a message stating that your bank account has been charged forty-seven dollars.

21. Reduced crime. In a cashless society, practically all physical crimes related to money—bank robberies, muggings, kidnappings, convenience-store holdups—will be eliminated. If banks have no money in the drawer, what is a bank robber going to say? "Transfer all your money into my personal account and here is my number"? Well, that still might happen, and if it does, he is sure to appear on the popular TV show, *The Dumbest Criminals.*

However, as I have stated earlier, cyber crimes will increase in a cashless society. You will probably not get mugged or murdered, but the potential for your bank account to be raided will rise.

22. Recovery of lost items. In a cashless society you will be able to find that lost shoe or CD in your house. Every item you purchase will come with an RFID tag that can beam a signal to readers located in every room in your house—and inform you exactly where the item is! In fact, you will be able to inventory every single item in your home with the push of one button. You will know how many bottles of shampoo and numbers of razors, shirts, videos, and books you have. You will not only be able to know the location, but also the replacement value of each item, and the total replacement value of everything in your house! You will even be able to find your car in the parking lot!

23. Non-forced compliance. In the initial stages of a cashless society, most institutions and businesses will use non-forced compliance to have people operate cashless. For example, the state of Illinois is using non-forced compliance for toll roads. They recently announced that those who pay cash at the tollgate will be charged twice as much as those who prepay and use a cashless I-PASS transponder device. No one is being "forced" to use the I-PASS, but you surely are penalized if you don't.

Anyone, anywhere, anytime

We will be living in a new global economy with immediate financial transactions being processed...

- from anyone

- located anywhere

- at any time.

Just look at the stated vision posted on Visa's Web site: "Visa's vision for the future of commerce is one in which buyers and sellers can conduct commerce securely and conveniently anywhere, anytime, and any way."[1]

Visa, MasterCard, other companies, governments, and institutions are fully committed to making this a reality in the fastest time frame possible. The world of cashless and global financial transactions is upon us. The cashless society is coming.

In the next chapter I will be answering the most asked question I've been hearing on this topic, *"What does the Bible say about a cashless society?"*

[1] http://corporate.visa.com/

CHAPTER 9

The Prophecy

Is a cashless society a sign of the end of the world?

IN THIS CHAPTER I WILL ATTEMPT to answer some of the most asked and most penetrating questions that relate specifically to a cashless society.

Very likely you have already thought of some of these questions. It is my sincere prayer and goal that my answers will be *biblical, logical,* and *succinct.*

The number one question people are asking me:

Is a cashless society a sign of the end of the world?

Who wouldn't want to know the answer to that question?

For me to answer this all-important question, I will need to answer a series of other questions such as:

- Does the Bible specifically say when the end of the world will come?

- Where do you find a cashless society in the Bible?

- Could we be required to have some form of a "mark" prior to the tribulation in order to buy and sell?

- What is the mark of the Beast, and how does it relate to a cashless society?

- Does the Bible give a general time frame of when we might expect a cashless society?

- What specific prophetic events should we be looking for that will precede the fulfillment of Revelation 13—the mark of the Beast?

- Should we always assume that a cashless society is anti-God?

- If I believe I will be raptured, why should I be concerned about a cashless society?

- Why is it so important for us to understand issues that relate to a cashless society?

Different Theological Perspectives

Before I begin answering the nine questions listed above, I must address a very important issue. I want you to know that I do not claim to have all the answers, and I acknowledge that some godly people hold to a different biblical theology about the last days. Since a cashless society would not be considered a major doctrinal issue, I pray and trust that we can have respect for one another, whatever view we hold concerning end times, and simply agree to disagree.

Now let's look at specific biblical questions that relate explicitly to the coming cashless society.

1. Does the Bible specifically say when the end of the world will come?

The Bible is clear that no one but the Father knows the exact time, but Jesus was clear that we will have signs (Mark 13:32). If you ever hear anyone saying he knows when the end of the world is going to take place, you know he is mistaken and should not be trusted!

So, our first question is easy to answer. No. The Bible does not specifically say when the end of the world will come.

2. Where do you find a cashless society in the Bible?

The specific words "cashless society" do not appear anywhere in the Bible. However, I believe that for Revelation 13:16–17 to be fulfilled, some type of a cashless system will be required.

Let's first read the passage, and then I will explain to you how I arrived at my conclusion.

> He also forced everyone, small and great, rich and poor, free and slave, to receive a mark on his right hand or on his forehead, so that no one could buy or sell unless he had the mark, which is the name of the beast or the number of his name. (Rev. 13:16–17 NIV)

Be sure to observe all the following points:

- **"He"** is an individual known as both the "second beast" and the "False Prophet" who has appeared on the world scene and uses a cashless economy to demand worship and allegiance to an already established world dictator, known in Scripture as the Beast or the Antichrist.

- **"Everyone"** includes *literally everyone in the world* who can buy and sell. However, some will refuse to receive the mark of the Beast on their body.

- **"Mark"** is some type of visible sign that will be noticeable to everyone. This mark will be either the name of the beast or the number of his name. That number is 666 (Revelation 13:17–18).

- **"Right hand or forehead"** is what the Bible gives as very specific locations. The mark must appear on the right hand or forehead—nowhere else.

Now, let me explain why I believe Revelation 13 requires a cashless society.

If any form of cash were still available, you would be able to buy and sell in secret. This specific system talked about in Revelation 13 will require the total elimination of cash, and all financial transactions will need to be made by someone who is "approved" to buy and sell in the secure global financial network.

If cash were still available, it would be impossible to control the buying and selling of goods in the world. However, if every man and woman had to use some form of an electronic means of payment (noncash), a person or institution could control his ability to buy or sell.

Therefore, in my opinion, all the evidence in Revelation 13:16–17 clearly points to the necessity of a *cashless society*.

However, some of my friends asked, **"What about bartering?"** Excellent question! Theoretically speaking, we can only assume that some form of bartering (the exchange of goods or services) will be taking place during this time of persecution. I believe bartering is the *only way* believers on the earth at that time will be able to obtain any goods or services for their family. (Though by refusing to take the mark, many of them will likely be put to death.)

3. Could we be required to have some form of a "mark" prior to the tribulation in order to buy and sell?

Yes. It is my opinion that just because the "mark" will be required during the last half of the tribulation (see question #5) to buy and sell *does not eliminate the possibility* that prior to the tribulation we will be required to have some form of mark or card or implanted computer chip to make financial transactions.

It is important to note that it is very possible that this earlier mark or card or computer chip might *not* be related in any way to the mark mentioned in Revelation 13.

However, I would become very concerned if this earlier mark were required to be put on your forehead or right hand. The Bible is very specific about the location of the mark of the Beast: your forehead or right hand.

4. What is the mark of the Beast, and how does it relate to a cashless society?

According to Revelation 13, those who do not take the mark of the Beast will not be able to buy food, pay for utilities, pay rent, or even buy gasoline!

Dr. Tim LaHaye in his book *Revelation Unveiled* provides his insights:

More important than the meaning is the use of these three numbers, 666. The False Prophet will use them as a means of forcing people to worship Antichrist. He will demand that everyone have his mark on their foreheads or on their hands in order to buy or sell. This economic pressure will be instrumental in causing many weak, worldly individuals to succumb to the establishment of this monarch, which will be tantamount to the personal rejection of Christ and acceptance of Antichrist. One can scarcely imagine the pressures of having to possess such a mark in order to secure the necessary food for his family. The U.S. government in World War II furnished a device of this kind in the form of food rationing. It was not enough to have money sufficient to pay for an item, for one had to have food stamps. The same will be true during the second half of the Tribulation, for the Antichrist will so control the economy that no one can live if he or she does not worship him.[1]

Scripture predicts that the coming world ruler will have complete control over the economy and that no one will be able to buy or sell without his permission (Revelation 13:7). A cashless society is a necessity for the last days.

5. Does the Bible give a general time frame of when we might expect a cashless society?

Today, we are literally seeing the groundwork being laid for the fulfillment of biblical prophecy. To understand better how a cashless society fits into prophecy, we must first take a look at the big picture of prophecy.

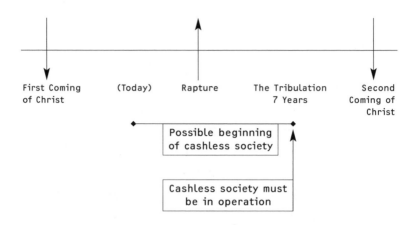

Let me explain some of the terms used.

First coming of Christ: when Christ was born in Bethlehem.

Rapture: when all believers (dead and alive) will be removed from earth and taken up to heaven. This marks the beginning of the seven-year tribulation period. The best-selling series "Left Behind" takes place after the rapture.

Tribulation: a period of seven years that will begin following the Rapture and continue until the second coming of Christ. At least part of this period will be a time of intense persecution of Christians by Antichrist and an outpouring of God's wrath.

It is at the midpoint of the Great Tribulation that I believe Revelation 13 will be fulfilled and a cashless society will be in operation.

Second coming of Christ: when Christ returns to earth not as a baby, but as the King of Kings and Lord of Lords.

6. What specific prophetic events should we be looking for that will precede the fulfillment of Revelation 13—the mark of the Beast?

The focus of this question is **other events** for which we should be watching, besides those big-picture events in the chart above, that signal the time is near when everyone will be required to take the mark of the Beast in order to be able to buy and sell.

Remember, as I stated earlier, we might be living in a cashless society before any of the following events take place.

- The first sign we might see is a **ten-nation** political and economic alliance forming (Daniel 7:7–8).

- Next, out of this newly formed ten-nation alliance, **a new world leader will emerge.** He will be respected around the world, exhibit supernatural power, and be controlled by Satan (Revelation 17:12–13).

- One of his first acts will be to **negotiate a peace covenant** on Israel's behalf—therefore bringing peace to the Middle East. This will be a welcome event in world history.

- The world dictator will receive a **fatal wound to his head** and **be miraculously healed** (Revelation 13:3). People from every nation will be amazed at his apparent resurrection from the dead.

- An individual known as the **False Prophet** will appear on the scene at the rebuilt temple in Jerusalem and declare that the world dictator (Antichrist/Beast) is god and must be worshiped by everyone in the world (Revelation 13:12).

- The Beast, a one-time peacemaker, will become an **evil dictator.** Turning his back on Israel and world peace, **he will break the peace covenant with Israel.**

- Finally, the False Prophet will create an image of the world dictator and require that **everyone worship the image** or be killed (Revelation 13:15). It is at this point that all will be required to **have a mark on their right hand or forehead** in order to buy or sell.

7. Should we always assume that a cashless society is anti-God?

Shortly before I did the final editing for this chapter, I was discussing the cashless society with my friend Jimmy, and he asked this question.

"Why do we naturally assume that having a cashless society is related to the end of the world or is something God does not want to happen?"

"WOW!" I thought to myself, *"Now that's a million-dollar question!"*

As I documented in chapter 5, there are many benefits to living in a cashless society. In chapters 3, 4, and 10, I documented the potential for evil in a cashless society. However, we must remember that living in a cashless society does not have to mean that evil people are in control. But we do know that one day, according to Revelation 13, evil people **will be** in control in what I expect will be a cashless world economy.

8. If I believe I will be raptured, why should I be concerned about a cashless society?

That is an excellent question. Let me answer it from two different perspectives:

If you are raptured before we have a cashless society, you are right; nothing matters.

If you are still on this earth and we have a cashless society, you should be on the alert for a system that in any way is linked to a world dictator or a requirement to take a mark on your forehead or right hand.

Finally, as a Christian, you should be using this fascinating topic as a tool to share Christ with others.

9. Why is it so important for us to understand issues that relate to a cashless society?

I can just hear someone asking, "Ethan, why are you making such a big deal about this?"

I will tell you, just as I told my friends, "Because, for the first time in history, the technology is in place for a cashless world economy."

Biblical prophecy is unfolding before our very eyes.

---

[1] Dr. Tim LaHaye, *Revelation Unveiled* (Grand Rapids, MI: Zondervan, 1999), 226–227.

· ·

CHAPTER 10

The Response

How can christians respond to concerns about a cashless society?

Let me begin this chapter by making a few recommendations.

- **Act like you knew it was coming.** There is no reason for you or anyone in your family or church to be caught off guard on this issue. You have a copy of this book, and it's my hope that, as a result of reading it, you understand the issues. You need not be caught unprepared.

- **Act intelligently.** Know your facts. Speak with conviction and intelligence. Be prepared to discuss this issue in your office, home, or at church.

- **Act responsibly.** Make good decisions. In the coming years, the level of risk will not diminish, but increase.

- **Alert, educate, and inform.** Tell as many people as possible what is about to happen, why it will happen, and the eternal consequences of anyone receiving the mark of the Beast.

- **Act godly.** Demonstrate a strong daily trust and faith in God.

Now let me answer more specific questions about a cashless society.

As christians, should we fight to stop the coming cashless society?

If given the opportunity to vote or voice my opinion, I would vote to retain the option to use cash. I believe the best scenario would be to take advantage of cashless for most transactions but still have the legal option to use cash if I desire to. This is a possible option. However, we expect there will be no cash during the events of Revelation 13. (See chapter 9 for more information.)

should i euer haue a computer chip implanted in my body?

As of today, I do not believe that an implanted computer chip is the mark of the Beast. Why? The mark of the Beast found in Revelation 13 appears to be some type of visible mark that will be noticeable to everyone.

However, I do believe that we should be cautious about implanting computer chips in our bodies. Too little is known at this time, but that will definitely change in the future. The invasion of privacy is my major concern at this point. When we become convinced that invasion of privacy is not an issue, an implanted chip might be something to seriously consider. That is, I might add, as long as you are *not required* to have it implanted in your right hand or forehead!

will believers be on the earth when all are required to take the mark of the beast?

No matter who is right or wrong concerning the Rapture, and who will be on earth during the Great Tribulation, this I do know. If you are on the earth when people are being forced to take the mark of the Beast—do not do it! Resist, even if it costs you your life! See next question for more information.

should a christian take the mark of the beast to be able to buy and sell?

No. The Bible teaches that it is the False Prophet who comes on the scene and requires that everyone worship the Antichrist (Beast) and receive the mark of the Beast on their right hand or forehead. It is the False Prophet who uses the cashless society to control people.

Those who do not agree to receive the mark of the Beast on their forehead or right hand will be persecuted. No one will be exempt. It will include the small and the great, the rich and the poor, the free and the slaves. Everyone in every nation will need the mark to make financial transactions.

The mark of the Beast will be a sign that you have pledged your allegiance to worship the Beast or world dictator. All the believers on the earth during that time should refuse to take the mark—no matter what the consequences.

Resist even if it costs you your life. Do not pledge your allegiance to anyone other than Christ. Those who take the mark of the Beast will have to bow the knee to the Antichrist.

what is the penalty for taking the mark?

"If any one worships the beast and his image, and receives a mark on his forehead or on his hand, he also will drink of the wine of the wrath of God, which is mixed in full strength in the cup of His anger; and he will be tormented with fire and brimstone in the presence of the holy angels and in the presence of the Lamb. And the smoke of their torment goes up forever and ever; and they have no rest day and night, those who worship the beast and his image, and whoever receives the mark of his name" (Revelation 14:9–11).

can christians survive in a cashless society?

It is very possible that we will have a cashless society before the Great Tribulation. Buying and selling should not be a problem. The only time a problem will arise is if an evil person takes control of the system or if we are living in the tribulation.

Persecution for those who come to Christ after the Rapture will be at the highest level. Yes, it will be difficult to survive, but God will give them His grace every day. Just like today in some countries, the church will have to go underground. Christians will have to live like an Acts 2 church when those who had possessions shared with those in need.

Christians during the tribulation can potentially survive for a while, but it will be with great persecution. Starvation and execution may continually threaten them. Just think how hard it would be to live if you could not make any financial transactions. People will experience persecution that this world has never seen before. The only way a Christian will be able to survive during a cashless society will be by bartering, exercising his faith, and living with an eternal perspective.

The writer of Hebrews understood this concept very well. In chapter 11 he listed many of the heroes of the faith and how they died.

> All these died in faith, without receiving the promises, but having seen them and having welcomed them from a distance, and having confessed that they were strangers and exiles on the earth.... But as it is, they desire a better country, that is a heavenly one. (vv. 13, 16)

How can anyone survive persecution? If you read the testimonies of prisoners of war, many have said you have to keep the faith and have hope for the future!

Are we living in the last days?

The Bible clearly says that no one knows when the end will come. We are to be on the alert and ready every day. See chapter 9 for a detailed answer.

How close are we to becoming a cashless society?

It would be foolish for me to set a specific date. As I documented in chapter 2, The Signs, we are gaining momentum in every area related to becoming cashless.

will we have any cash in a cashless society?

I believe we will have limited cash for a number of years, but eventually all cash will disappear. Why would the government want to keep printing it and fighting against counterfeiters and crime if e-currency were available? I realize that some will protest, but I believe the government will eventually remove all paper and coin money from circulation.

for a cashless society to work, will the world need to have one currency?

No, with computers able to calculate exchange rates, one currency will not be necessary. Most would agree that the euro will gain strength and popularity in the latter days, but the world will not have to operate on one currency.

is a 100 percent cashless society technologically possible in our world?

Yes, we have the computer power to operate a cashless economy. A global economy is not unrealistic. However, before we can enter into a global cashless economy, we will need the ability to make wireless transactions from any part of the world. (See the section on "global hot spot" in chapter 2.)

is all the hype about a cashless society for nothing?

Currently there is not much "hype" about a cashless society, because we have the option to make financial transactions with cash or cashless. However, as the government moves more toward cashless, and as businesses begin penalizing you for each cash transaction, the noise will begin to escalate.

is the cashless society the result of a conspiracy or simply technological progression?

I have seen no evidence pointing to any conspiracy. I believe what we are seeing is the combination of (a) advancing technology, (b) incentive for businesses to make more money, and (c) fulfillment of prophecy.

what will be the primary payment method in a cashless society? Biometrics, debit cards, implantable chips, cell phones, internet, or a combination of all?

It is impossible to know the answer at this time. However, it is my opinion that the payment vehicle will use some form of biometrics for verification—like iris scans, fingerprints, or hand scans.

Implantable computer chips also appear to be an option. The problem with cards or jewelry is they can be lost or stolen.

who will be the key players in making a cashless society a reality?

Obviously the government is the key player, because it is the only institution that has the power to remove currency from circulation. Other key players are the major credit card companies.

will a cashless society make my financial transactions safer, or will it create greater risk?

Overall, your financial transactions should be safer. But, risk will still be a factor. The advanced forms of payment vehicles and biometric verification will help secure each transaction. I believe that in the future we will have the ability to be informed when a financial transaction hits our account. This could be in the form of a text message to our cell phone or watch.

Are bankers and the united states government in favor of a cashless society?

It does appear that financial institutions and the government are in favor of a cashless society. Cashless means less administration, less expense, and more income.

whom will it affect?

Everyone.

what is the definition of a cashless society?

We will be a cashless society when the government removes 100 percent of the currency from circulation.

is all the talk of the coming cashless society just another Y2K phenomenon? if not, tell me specifically why not.

I believe cashless is different from Y2K for this reason: Y2K was based on a lot of speculation and a specific date and time. "What might happen at midnight?" "Will the computer work?" Cashless will be gradual and is a work in progress. The hype will come when the government begins discussing the advantages of removing all our currency from circulation.

is the cashless society morally right or wrong?

I would say that "cashless" is neutral until it becomes directly connected with the Beast in Revelation 13. Cashless can be used for good and evil. Technology is not evil, but evil men can use technology for evil.

specifically, what is the mark of the Beast found in Revelation 13? will it be like a tattoo, on top of skin, under skin, or could it be a computer chip?

As I mentioned earlier in this chapter, I believe the mark will be some type of a visible sign noticeable to everyone.

e-Tithing

What about e-tithing? Is this contrary to Scripture?

There is no doubt that e-tithing will create controversy in churches across America. As thousands of churches have already signed up to offer e-tithing, thousands of others are considering it. Let me try to add some perspective for those trying to decide what to do.

Obviously, Scripture does not specifically address e-tithing. However, some could have the opinion that e-tithing is tied to the mark of the Beast. They are automatically assuming that anything cashless is anti-God, which does not have to be the case. I personally cannot make such a direct connection unless the members are required to have some type of mark on their right hand or forehead before they can e-tithe.

What about spontaneous giving during worship?

Just because a family signs up to e-tithe does not mean that they cannot give spontaneously. If you are sitting in a worship service and God prompts you to be financially involved in a project, you can still drop cash or a check in the plate—that is, until the move to a completely cashless economy.

Should churches split over this issue?

Absolutely not! If leadership decides to offer e-tithing, let the members decide whether they want to participate or not. Don't make this issue a bigger deal than it needs to be. If you want to be involved, sign up. If you don't want to give electronically, don't sign up. I believe that leadership should not aggressively try to market or persuade members to sign up for e-tithing.

What about churches taking credit card donations?

Let me answer this question by saying that I believe debit transactions are the best way to go. A debit transaction transfers money directly from your bank account into the church's bank account. The problem with credit card donations is the potential for a member to make a donation and not have the ability to pay the credit card company in full at the end of the month. Now the church has become an accomplice to the member living in financial bondage.

No, it is not the church's fault, but they were involved in the transaction that eventually led to financial bondage.

What are your options?

If you are 100 percent opposed to e-tithing, what will you do when we literally have a cashless global economy? Not give at all? If that is the case, what is a church to do when that happens? Close the doors? No!

We must remember that technological advances should not be the theological focus. Money, checks, debit cards, and electronic transactions are morally neutral. They are neither good nor evil on their own. Money can be used for good and for evil, but money in itself is neither good nor evil.

Our only concern in using a cashless economy should be if we are required to worship anyone but God. It is only at that juncture that the system has become evil and we must not participate! No exceptions!

The controversy concerning e-tithing is very low right now but will increase as more churches offer and begin aggressively promoting electronic giving. Most churches can eliminate controversy if they do not aggressively market electronic giving. They can offer it but not campaign for everyone to use it. When we have a cashless society, church members will not even have an option to write a check or drop cash in the offering plate. The only option will become some form of an electronic gift—or not to give at all.

Finally, whether you are a major proponent or major opponent of e-tithing, let me exhort you not to let Satan use this issue to create division within your church. We must stand united for the cause of Christ.

Finally, what should be your spiritual attitude concerning a cashless society?

Be alert!

Let me strongly encourage you to stay informed about the coming cashless society. Study your Bible, read current events, pray, and trust God every day. We are not to fear (2 Timothy 1:7) nor are we to be anxious (Philippians 4:6). We are instructed to be "strong in the Lord, and in the strength of His might" (Ephesians 6:10).

Should I be worried about a cashless society?

The Bible says to be anxious for nothing (Philippians 4:6–8), and that would include a cashless society.

Our future is in God's control. We should not fear the future but embrace it. We should not fear persecution, but if it comes we should ask for God's mercy and grace. God is looking for faithful men and women who are devoted to living wholeheartedly for Him. (See 2 Chronicles 16:9.)

Throughout the centuries, God has used persecution to purge the faithless and reveal the faithful. Any type of future persecution that might come will be no different. The faithless will take the easy path, while the faithful will stand firm.

If we ever have to face that day, let us remember how the heroes of the faith responded:

Who by faith conquered kingdoms, performed acts of righteousness, obtained promises, shut the mouths of lions, quenched the power of fire, escaped the edge of the sword, from weakness were made strong, became mighty in war, put foreign armies to flight. Women received back their dead by resurrection; and others were tortured, not accepting their release, so that they might obtain a better resurrection; and others experienced mockings, and scourgings, yes, also chains and imprisonment. They were stoned, they were sawn in two, they were tempted, they were put to death with the sword; they went about in sheepskins, in goatskins, being destitute, afflicted, ill-treated (men of whom the world was not worthy), wandering in deserts and mountains and caves and holes in the ground. And all these, having gained approval through their faith, did not receive what was promised, because God had provided something better for us, so that apart from us they would not be made perfect. (Hebrews 11:33–40)

No matter how difficult life might become, keep the faith! **Keep the faith!** For we are only strangers and exiles on this earth, simply passing through to a better land.

Whether we're in a cash or cashless economy, "not one of us lives for himself, and not one dies for himself; for if we live, we live for the Lord, or if we die, we die for the Lord; therefore whether we live or die, we are the Lord's" (Romans 14:7–8).

Press on.

· ·

CHAPTER 11

The Two Worlds

Are you ready for another world without money?

When it's time for "Cashing It In"... will you be ready for another kind of world that functions completely without money?

This time I am not talking about the coming cash-less society on earth, but about something far more significant: *getting ready for heaven.*

Yes, the title and subtitle of this book have a subtle double meaning. I firmly believe that one day we will be living in a cashless society. And equally as true for all of us, there will come a day when we will literally cash it in—when we die! On that day, we will have lost the ability to control our assets, adjust our portfolios, or even support the kingdom of God.

The Bible says, "It is appointed for men to die once and after this comes judgment" (Hebrews 9:27).

Responding to these biblical truths about death and heaven demands a deeper level of thinking—a level of thinking that goes beyond the sometimes insignificant decisions we make each day. As important as it is for us to plan for a cashless society on this earth, this preparation is trivial compared to the significance of our decisions concerning the world to come.

For in the case of death we are talking about eternal consequences!

We are talking about irrevocable outcomes.

We are talking about results that will last forever.

You might be thinking, *How do I get ready for a world (heaven) without money?*

There are specific things the Bible tells us we should be doing. Space does not allow me to list them all, but here are some of the most important.

The first thing is to be sure that you are going to heaven.

Jesus once told a man named Nicodemus, "Truly, truly, I say to you, unless one is born again he cannot see the kingdom of God" (John 3:3).

Then Nicodemus asked, "How can a man be born when he is old? He cannot enter a second time into his mother's womb and be born, can he?" (John 3:4).

Jesus answered, "Truly, truly, I say to you, unless one is born of water and the Spirit he cannot enter into the kingdom of God. That which is born of the flesh is flesh; and that which is born of the Spirit is spirit" (John 3:5-6).

Do you want to go to heaven?

Jesus said there are two requirements:

- You must be born of water.
- You must be born of the Spirit.

BORN OF WATER

To be born of water or flesh is to have experienced a physical birth. Obviously, everyone who is reading this has already completed the first requirement—to be physically born—of water.

BORN OF THE SPIRIT

But, the greatest question is, have you experienced a spiritual birth?

WHY MUST YOU BE BORN SPIRITUALLY?

Romans 5:12 says, "Therefore, just as through one man sin entered into the world, and death through sin, and so death spread to all men, because all sinned."

Since the fall of Adam and Eve, every person is born into this world spiritually dead and with a sinful nature. Without God's Spirit, we cannot be spiritually alive. Romans 3:23 says, "For all have sinned and fall short of the glory of God." Ephesians 2:1 tells us, "And you were dead in your trespasses and sins ..."

Did you notice your position? Dead—that is spiritually dead.

Think about it this way. Every person born into the world since Adam and Eve has a physical body (born of water), but according to Romans 5:12 every person born has a "dead spirit."

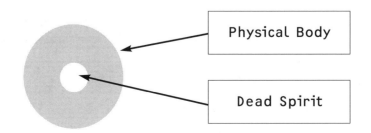

Physical Body

Dead Spirit

The outer circle represents the fact that we all have a physical body, while the inner circle represents the fact that at birth our spirit is dead. To put it another way, at birth we have a *spiritual vacuum or void* in our lives.

If everyone is born into this world with a dead spirit, how then can a person make that spirit alive and be born again and enter the kingdom of God?

We find the answer to this question in John 1:12–13, "But as many as received Him [Jesus], to them He gave the right to become children of God, . . . who were born not of blood, nor of the will of the flesh nor of the will of man, but of God."

Notice a spiritual birth is **not based on** family relationships or your family heritage (not of blood). It is not based on all your good deeds (nor of the will of the flesh) or what any person or religious leader has to say about you (nor of the will of man). It's not a human accomplishment. Only God can grant spiritual birth.

To whom does God grant spiritual birth?

To as many as received Him (Jesus), to them He gave the right to become the children of God (John 1:12–13).

To receive Jesus simply means to accept Him. It conveys the idea of believing in Him and receiving His gift of salvation. How does a person accept Jesus into his or her life?

Ephesians 2:8–9 says, "For by grace you have been saved through faith; and that not of yourselves, it is the gift of God; not as a result of works, so that no one may boast." (To be "saved" is to be spiritually born again.)

Let's examine several of the words in these two verses:

For by grace...

The word *grace* means you have been granted the ability to receive a gift of salvation you do not deserve.

For example, if I were to place a beautiful diamond ring in my open hand and say, "I want to give you this beautiful ring. You cannot buy it, work for it, or earn it in any way. It is my free gift to you. The only thing you have to do is ask for it and receive it," this is exactly what God says in relation to being born again (saved).

...through faith...

It is by faith, believing in Jesus and what He has done for you, that you receive His gift of salvation.

...not a result of works, so that no one may boast

Being born again and going to heaven is not based on any of your good works! Being born again is not based on attending church, church membership, baptism, giving money for good causes, doing good deeds, or anything else you might think of trying to do to find favor with God. Being born again is not a matter of calculating, "Do I have more good deeds than bad deeds?"

We cannot ignore what Jesus specifically said about salvation in John 14:6: "I am the way, and the truth, and the life; no one comes to the Father, but through Me." He did not say, "No one comes to the Father unless you have enough good works."

But, many have said and you might be thinking, "I've been a good person all my life. Surely God will let me enter His kingdom."

Good logic, but bad theology ...

If you are placing your trust in your good works, *you have not received* God's **free gift** of salvation through Jesus Christ. Because God says it's impossible to work for your salvation—you must simply receive it as a gift (Ephesians 2:8–9) by trusting in Jesus alone. It is *His* work of dying on the cross *in our place for our sins* that makes salvation possible for us. We just need to trust and believe in Him, rather than in anything we have done.

Many people will end up dying and spending eternity separated from God, simply because they are *depending upon their good works for salvation.* If you place any trust or faith in your good works, you will be greatly surprised, and I might add disappointed, when you stand before the Lord on judgment day.

Being **born again** is the most important thing a person will ever do in life. There is absolutely no close second! Money, family, careers, and awards are all important, but none of these things will ever be as significant as receiving and welcoming Christ into your life. If you have never been born again, the Bible says that you are destined to spend eternity in hell separated from God.

Obviously, if you are reading this, you have completed the first part of the requirements to see the kingdom of God—born of water. However, have you been born of the spirit?

What is your answer to this question?

If you don't know, you can make sure right now by praying and receiving or welcoming Jesus into your life. Below you will find a suggested prayer. There is nothing special about the following prayer; it's simply a prayer to help you express the desire of your heart.

"Lord Jesus, I need You and believe in You. By faith I receive You into my life and trust only in You for salvation from eternal punishment for my sins. Please forgive all my sins. I acknowledge that my spirit is dead. It is my heart's desire to be spiritually born again. Thank You for giving me an opportunity to be a child of God and a member of Your family. Amen."

If you have placed your faith and trust in Christ alone, as this prayer expresses, you have been **spiritually born again and are destined to spend eternity in heaven!**

The second thing that comes to mind in preparation for heaven is that we need to live with a biblical framework that is taught in 1 Timothy 6:7. "For we have brought nothing into the world, so we cannot take anything out of it either." When you get right down to it—life is very simple. We bring nothing in; we take nothing out.

What does this mean to believers? Acknowledge that God owns it all (Psalm 24:1), and we are simply stewards of His possessions (Luke 16:10–13). Like Job, hold your material possessions loosely. Immediately after Job lost everything he owned, we find him saying, "The LORD gave and the LORD has taken away. Blessed be the name of the LORD" (Job 1:21).

I believe it was Billy Graham who said, "I have never seen a hearse pulling a U-Haul." *There is a lot of theology in that statement!*

Third, as we prepare for heaven, we must acknowledge that wealth is worthless on judgment day. Proverbs 11:4 (NLT) says, "Riches won't help on the day of judgment." All the assets that you have accumulated on earth will be of no value as you stand before the judgment seat of Christ. In one sense, you will be penniless as you stand before God. The powerful currency of this world will be of no value to you or anyone else on judgment day and in the world to come.

Remember what Jesus taught us in Matthew 16:26? "What profit is it to a man if he gains the whole world, and loses his own soul?" (NKJV).

The answer: nothing.

It profits him *absolutely nothing* in the **world to come,** even if he owns the whole world today but does not know Christ as Savior!

The fourth way to prepare for the coming world without money is to be a generous giver while you are still alive! In Matthew 6:19–21, Jesus gives us the best advice about preparing for heaven. "Do not store up for yourselves treasures on earth, where moth and rust destroy, and where thieves break in and steal. But store up for yourselves treasures in heaven, where neither moth nor rust destroys and where thieves do not break in or steal; for where your treasure is, there will your heart be also."

In one aspect, being a generous giver while on this earth is one of the best ways to get ready for a world without money. Jesus could not have made it any simpler! The more you give while on earth (cash or e-cash), the more treasures you will have in heaven.

We must also remember that God's accounting is different from man's accounting. For in God's economy, a poor widow who can only give a few thousand dollars during a lifetime in reality can give proportionately more than the successful businessman who has given millions of dollars during his life (Mark 12:42–44). Don't focus on how much you are giving *compared to others;* focus on what God has entrusted to you and what proportion you will use to support God's kingdom.

Finally, let me summarize what I have said.

There are **two worlds** (heaven and earth), **two economies** (God's and the world's), and **one** very important question. That essential question is: Are you really ready for a world without money?

I pray that you are.

# the updates

How can I keep up-to-date on critical issues concerning the cashless society?

WWW.FOUNDATIONSFORLIVING.ORG
New developments relating to the coming cashless society are happening just about every day. On our Web site, I will keep you updated with developments as they unfold.

We are planning to offer the following on our Web site:

- Important Web site links
- New developments
- New resources
- Bulletin board for you to post your thoughts and questions
- Updated articles from Ethan
- Additional documentation that was not published in this book

Go to **www.foundationsforliving.org** for the most updated information.

The cashless
Time Line

352 BC	Romans may have invented the check.
1500s	In Holland, checks first got widespread usage and later spread to England.
1681	In the United States, checks are said to have first been used when cash-strapped businessmen in Boston mortgaged their land to a fund, against which they could write checks.
1700	The word *check* also may have originated in England in the 1700s when serial numbers were placed on these pieces of paper as a way to keep track of, or "check" on them.
1762	The first printed checks are traced to 1762 and British banker Lawrence Childs.
1781	First bank in U.S. was established—Bank of North America.
1932	Americans were required to turn in all gold to government.
1944	International Monetary Fund was established.

1945	United Nations began.
1958	Bank of America released its blue, white, and gold BankAmericard.
1966	MasterCard was created.
1969	First ATM machine.
1970s	Local and regional banks introduced debit cards.
Early 70s	Prepaid cards beginning to be offered.
1971	Gold no longer backs U.S. dollar.
1973	Automated Clearing House (ACH) founded. Manages the clearing of electronic payments for participating financial institutions.
6/16/74	First commercial scanning of a Universal Product Code (UPC) of a ten-pack of Wrigley's chewing gum.
1975	Visa introduced their first debit card.
1976	BankAmericard changes its name to VISA.
1986	Visa begins to offer multiple-currency clearing for transactions.
1986	IRS offers e-filing for tax returns.
1994	Internet broker accounts become popular.
1995	Visa five-year debit card educational campaign begins.
1995	Use of paper checks peaks. Has declined every year since 1995.

1995	Rapid growth and use of Internet.
1997	First U-Scan checkout line machine available.
3/13/97	U.S. Patent office registered patent number 5,629,678 for a Personal Tracking and Recovery System.
1997	MobilExxon introduces SpeedPass cashless pay-at-the-pump option.
1999	U.S Department of Treasury's EFT'99 initiative—goal to increase the number of federal payments made electronically.
2001	MasterCard launches the mc2 Card, the first non-rectangular card.
9/11/01	Terrorists attack United States.
9/12/01	We begin living in a post 9/11 world.
9/16/01	The first person to receive the VeriChip was Dr. Richard Seelig, a New Jersey surgeon.
5/10/02	Jacombs family received VeriChip on *Today* show, on National TV.
2003	Fast-food establishments begin to expand cashless payment options.
2003	ACH clears more than ten billion transactions in one year.
2003	Consumer debt passes two trillion dollars for first time in history.

The cashless Time line

2003	We are seeing a significant rise in non-cash payments for purchases less than five dollars—called micropayments.
2003	Debit cards in circulation reach over one billion.
6/03	Wal-Mart announced it would require its top one hundred suppliers to begin shipping RFID-tagged pallets and cases by January 2005.
2004	First Data completed its merger with Concord.
4/30/04	Wal-Mart begins receiving cases and pallets with RFID tags at a distribution center in Dallas/Fort Worth.
10/04	Check 21 Act—allows banks to replace paper checks with an electronic version of the check.
2004	Several major retail chains mandate use of RFID tags.
2004	Use of biometrics in passports increases.
2004	Several NFL stadiums begin to offer cashless payment options.
2004	MasterCard announces they have more than 200 million smart cards globally.
2004	Cashless vending machines are becoming more popular due to better technology.
2004	Global debit transactions surpass global credit transactions.

2004	E-tithing is beginning to be promoted in many churches.
2004	Over half of tax returns are being filed electronically.
12/7/04	Salvation Army begins accepting debit and credit cards at select bell-ringing locations in Arizona.
2005	E911 Mandate—by the end of 2005 all cell phones must include GPS device that can pinpoint your exact location.
2006	Projected that all fast-food establishments will be offering cashless payment options.
Future	Virtual cashless (with some cash remaining).
Future	Cashless society.
Future	Rapture of believers.
Future	Seven years of tribulation.
Future	People are required to have mark of Beast to buy and sell.
Future	Second return of Christ.

 # GLOSSARY

ACH: Automated Clearing House; handles electronic transactions for direct deposit and auto-pay. For more information go to www.nacha.org.

Active technology: Requires interaction of some form for each electronic transaction. For example, you have to swipe your card or punch in your PIN or type in your card number.

Alert: To warn of a coming event that has potential for harm or danger; not to alarm.

Antivirus software: Software designed to quarantine, delete, or prevent a destructive computer virus from attacking your computer or network.

ATM: Automatic Teller Machine; allows you to withdraw cash, check balances, and make transfers.

Biometrics: The use of fingerprints, iris scans, or a number of other personal identification means. Other examples: hand geometry, voice, gait, signature recognition, thermal imaging.

Cashless society: When no cash or coins will be used to make a financial transaction.

Check 21 Act: Went into effect October 28, 2004. This new law allows banks to replace paper checks with an electronic version of the check.

Check card: Same as debit card; see debit card.

Contactless payment: The ability to make a purchase or payment without having to physically touch any device. Contactless payment devices are used for toll roads and some gasoline pumps.

Cracker: (See also Hacker) A cracker's goal is to crack secure systems, generally with criminal intent—in contrast to a hacker who generally tries to enter a system to obtain data or to play a prank. Both acts of unauthorized intrusion are crimes.

Cyber crimes: A criminal act when computers, the Internet, or networks are used to commit a crime. Also known as hacking. Examples are Internet fraud, identity theft, bank account theft, and credit card theft. Cyber crimes are not physical crimes but are committed by using a computer and the Internet or a corporate network. In a cashless society, cyber crimes will increase.

Debit card: Debit cards are linked directly to a bank account. They can be used to make purchases at a store or over the Internet and withdraw cash from an ATM. They function just like a check, except that funds are immediately withdrawn from your checking account. Sometimes called a check card.

Direct deposit: When funds are deposited directly into your account. You do not receive a physical check to deposit.

E-Cash: Electronic cash.

E-Commerce: The buying and selling of merchandise on the Internet or with some type of electronic transaction not involving the use of cash.

E-Filing: Filing your taxes without the use of paper.

E-Tithing: Giving to a church or ministry by electronic funds transfer.

ETA: Electronic Transfer Account.

EFT: Electronic Funds Transfer.

EFTA: The Electronic Funds Transfer Act is a federal consumer protection law covering electronic transactions. It covers electronic fund transfer products such as bank accounts, debit cards, ATMs, and Internet banking.

EPCs: Electronic Product Codes.

Euro: Common currency being used in European nations.

Firewall: Software designed to prevent unauthorized access to your personal computer or a computer network. Designed to help prevent hackers or crackers from accessing your computer system.

Generation Y: Those born 1979–1994. The second largest generation in U.S. history—an estimated 60 million people—who are currently finishing high school and college. (Baby boomers, born from 1946–1964, are over 70 million. Generation X, born 1965–1978, is only 17 million.)

Global hot spot: Not available today. In the future you will have the ability to connect to the Internet or perform financial transactions from literally any location in the world. (See Hot spot.)

GPS: Global Positioning System—a group of 28 satellites orbiting the earth. GPS is used by the military, OnStar, and numerous others.

Hacker/Hacking: (See Cracker) Someone who achieves unauthorized access to a computer or system.

Hot spot: Usually a heavily populated location (airport, library, college campus, hotel) that allows a wireless Internet connection.

Identity theft: When someone steals and uses your identity—9.3 million people in the U.S. were affected by some form of identity theft in 2004.

Implantable chips: Small computer chips that can be inserted into the body that provide health or financial data.

Internet banking: Use of the Internet to make purchases, order checks, pay bills, or transfer funds.

Mark of the Beast: Some type of visible sign that will be placed on a person's right hand or forehead. Whoever receives the mark will be tormented forever (Revelation 14:11).

Micropayments: Payments or purchases that are less than five dollars.

Payroll cards: Cards that are used to pay employees. Employers deposit employee wages into the cards, and then they can be used like debit cards.

Phishing: A scam in which e-mail is sent requesting the recipient to click on a Web site link and provide private information such as a Social Security number. The e-mail appears to be from a reputable company or financial institution asking the recipient to update his or her file.

POS: Point of sale.

Post 9/11 world: How we think and live after the terrorist attack on September 11, 2001.

Prepay cards: Money can be stored on a card and used in restaurants or to make purchases. The most common prepay card is a gift card.

Pre-authorized debits: Pre-authorized debits allow customers to have regular, recurring bills automatically paid on a specific date. For example, each month you could have your car payment automatically paid out of your checking account to the lender.

Prophecy: Prediction of future events.

Rapture: When all believers (dead and alive) will be removed from earth and taken up to heaven.

Regulation E (Electronic Fund Transfers): Federal Reserve Board requirement that a written receipt be provided showing the date, amount, and location of each transfer. It must also show any service fees as a result of the transaction.

RFID: Radio Frequency Identification tags. Tags can be passive or active. A passive tag requires a reader to activate it, while an active tag does not need activation.

Secure Web site: Uses SSL (or Secure Socket Layer) and encrypting data to transfer data over the Internet in a coded or secret message. Most secure Web sites will have the following in their address: https:www. Note the "s" following the http.

Smart card: Card that has an imbedded small computer chip that can store names, financial data, passwords, and even e-cash.

Spam: Unsolicited electronic junk mail. Usually sent to thousands of e-mail addresses at one time.

U-commerce: Universal or ubiquitous commerce with no barriers of time, currency, geography, or access.

URL: Uniform Resource Locator—the Web address that routes you to a specific Web site. For example the URL for Foundations for Living is www.foundationsforliving.org.

U-Scan: Device in stores that allows you to check yourself out.

Virus: Usually loaded onto your computer when you receive an e-mail (with a virus). A computer virus can reproduce, slow down a computer, destroy the contents of your hard drive, cause your computer to do strange things like turn off and on, and spread to other computers.

ABOUT THE AUTHOR

ETHAN POPE is president of Foundations for Living, a ministry dedicated to helping people simplify and clarify life issues from a biblical and practical perspective. He is a graduate of Dallas Theological Seminary and a CERTIFIED FINANCIAL PLANNER™ professional, though he has never had a financial planning practice. Ethan is an author, speaker, and regular guest on national radio programs. His primary field of expertise is the theological and practical aspects of managing money.

Other books by Ethan Pope include *How to Be a Smart Money Manager, There's No Place Like Home, Creating Your Personal Money MAP,* and *The Personal Finance Course.*

Ethan and his wife, Janet, have two adult children and live in Hattiesburg, Mississippi.

CONTACTING ETHAN POPE

FOR INFORMATION ON:

- Inviting Ethan Pope to speak in your city or church
- Ordering resources online
- Attending a Foundations For Living seminar in your area
- Receiving Foundations For Living publications

Visit our Web site:

www.foundationsforliving.org

Or write to:

Ethan Pope
Foundations For Living
P.O. Box 15356
Hattiesburg, MS 39404

601-582-2000

CASHING IT IN TEAM

ACQUIRING EDITOR
Greg Thornton

COPY EDITOR
Allan Sholes

BACK COVER COPY
Laura Pokrzywa

COVER & INTERIOR DESIGN
The DesignWorks Group, Inc.
www.thedesignworksgroup.com

PRINTING AND BINDING
Versa Press, Inc.

The typeface for the text of this book is
StempelSchneidler